The Group Workshop Way in the Church

Other Books by the Same Author

PAUL F. DOUGLASS

The
Group
Workshop
Way
in the
Church

Visuals by
MARY ELEANOR SPEAR

Association
Press
NEW YORK

THE GROUP WORKSHOP WAY IN THE CHURCH

Copyright © 1956 by
National Board of Young Men's Christian Associations

Association Press, 291 Broadway, New York, N.Y. 10007

Fifth Printing, 1964

Library of Congress catalog card number: 56-10967

Printed in the United States of America

To

GEORGE C. WILLIAMS

who shares the aims and aspirations of others
and helps in their fulfillment

PREFACE

One night a pastor came home from a meeting of the Men's Brotherhood. "You know," he said to his wife, "I've been making an inventory of what I do. Aside from my pastoral calling and sermon preparation, almost my whole time is spent in getting ready for meetings or attending them. I keep asking myself whether the group must not offer a main avenue of the ministry to stir people to undergo inner growth toward spiritual maturity."

In eighteen words Professor Herbert A. Thelen, director of the Human Dynamics Laboratory, University of Chicago, says to this minister in substance, "Yes, your suspicion is scientifically correct." Listen: "The face-to-face group working on a problem is the meeting ground of the individual personality and society."[1] Professor Thelen goes on to say that "without social purposes shared with others there would be no basis for the give-and-take through which the individual develops his capabilities, and without the difference among individual personalities there would be no basis for the creation of new and better solutions to the problems of living."[2]

This book therefore talks about the spiritual growth which it is possible for people to experience when they are participants with others in the work of the church. The study ties together current findings in group dynamics, social psychology, human relations, cultural anthropology, and administration with Christian ideas of man. It attempts to provide a clearer insight into one of the avenues of an effective ministry.

The Second Assembly of the World Council of Churches spoke of the introversion of the average congregation, of its concern for its own worship comfort, its own budget prosperity, and its own social solidarity. The workshop church is one way of overcoming "routine" Christianity. It places the accent on outlook and upreach of the human being as he learns

vii

by doing in the company of others. The workshop concept looks at the church as a fellowship to help people grow spiritually, and "in the doing" to share their religious experiences with others; for experience, as Professor Thelen says, "is an active process of working with others for common goals."[3] It is educative "to the extent that it involves thinking about what one is doing, why he is doing it, and the general significance, usefulness, and applicability of the methods he is using in doing it."[4] The workshop church is a demonstration laboratory of Christian belief in action. It is, as Paul Scherer once said, "theology on an errand."

People crave activity which brings them into warm, congenial, purposeful relationships with others and gives them goals that challenge their whole existence. One day Professor Gordon Allport, chairman of the Department of Psychology, Harvard University, was asked how people could be encouraged to play more active roles. "I have one suggestion," he replied. "Ask people to take on participant duties!"[5] Jesus operated in just this way. He took the initiative to invite specific persons to do particular jobs. He walked up to Simon and Andrew while they were at work and said to them in substance: "I have a role for you to play" . . . and "straightway they . . . followed him."[6] He came upon James and John while they were in their ship mending their nets. "And . . . they followed him."[7] Going down the road he saw Matthew collecting taxes. "And he . . . followed him."[8] Jesus extended personal invitations. He proposed active roles in a program directed toward the achievement of heartfelt goals. To his disciples he proposed teamwork which was goal-oriented, task-centered, and God-related.

The title of this book developed in a conversation in the library of the S. S. *Queen Elizabeth* as I sat visiting with John R. Mott. He was making his last crossing from London to New York. "Douglass," he said,

> I have spent my life attending meetings. I think perhaps I have had the privilege of sitting in more meetings in more places with more different kinds of people over more years than any living man. I have presided over more assemblies, chaired more committees, led more informal conferences, and been a party to more intimate

heart-to-heart conversations than any other American.
Over the decades I have developed deep convictions
about the power of meetings to change personal lives and
to change the world. There is power in the process of
thinking common problems through together, participating in planning programs of action, and performing
assignments under the motivation of high spiritual mission. From my experience I have come to look upon the
meeting as a superlative social invention for human communication, and sharing of social purposes, getting work
done, and—note this—for changing one's self, others, and
the world. *The church is actually a group workshop.*

This book takes its title from that description of the meeting
as given on that voyage by John R. Mott. It needs to be pointed
out that the word "workshop" is used literally in the context
of this book. The workshop is merely a place where people do
work—where human beings exert their strength and faculties to
accomplish a purpose. Thus the connotation of the word differs
from the term as used in the field of education.

In organization, the chapter sequence divides naturally into three parts. Part I discusses the theory and mechanics of the
church operating as a group workshop. Part II deals with the
dynamics of spiritual growth in groups. Part III summarizes the
discussion and points an ongoing direction. Chapter by chapter
this book explains fundamental principles and studies them as
they operate in specific church program situations. The case
histories, of course, merely illustrate the development of the
thesis of the volume. They show how the principles can be
and are being applied. They do not attempt to suggest a church
program. They serve only to indicate how representative
churches effectively employ the techniques in an enriched
ministry. Thus the case history material serves only as a guide
to point a direction and light a path.

In the development of this study the work of Professor Herbert A. Thelen has been a source of great help. The rich mem-
ories of association with the late John R. Mott have been a
constant force in the writing of the manuscript. I wish to express my personal appreciation of these two leaders of thought
and action.

This book reports good news to people who work with peo-

ple. It tells what social scientists have discovered about how
human beings grow as spiritual selves as they work together
wholeheartedly in purposeful activity. It shows how the group
can serve as a vehicle for deepening Christian experience. In
the refining interactions of group participation in God-related,
goal-oriented, and task-centered activity, the person grows "in
wisdom and stature and in favor with God and man."

PAUL DOUGLASS

ACKNOWLEDGMENTS

Grateful acknowledgment is made to the following:

Adult Education Association of the United States for materials adapted from *Adult Leadership*.

American Bar Association for quotation from the *Journal* by Judge Julius H. Miner.

American Management Association for quotation from *General Electric's Philosophy and Approach for Management Development* by Harold F. Smiddy.

Association Press for quotations from *Religious Beliefs of Youth* by Murray G. Ross and *How to Be a Modern Leader* by Lawrence K. Frank.

Beacon Press for quotations from *Explorations in Altruistic Love and Behavior*, edited by Pitrim A. Sorokin.

Foster and Stewart for quotation from *Dynamics of Learning* by Nathaniel Cantor.

General Electric Company for quotations from *Integrating and Motivating for Effective Performance* by Harold F. Smiddy.

Harper & Brothers for quotations from *Human Factors in Management*, edited by Schuyler Dean Hoslett; *The Holy Bible* translated by James Moffatt.

Harvard University Press for quotations from *Toward a General Theory of Action* by Talcott Parsons and Edward A. Shils; and *Unraveling Juvenile Delinquency* by Sheldon and Eleanor Glueck.

John Knox Press for quotations from *A Call to Faith* by Rachel Henderlite.

Methodist Publishing House for quotation from *Leaders of Young People* by Frank Wade Smith.

McGraw-Hill Book Company for quotations from *The Psychodynamics of Abnormal Behavior* by J. F. Brown.

National Council of Churches for quotations from *Improving the Total Program of Your Church*.

New American Library of World Literature for quotation from *The Holy Bible in Brief*, edited by James Reeves.

Ohio State University Press for quotations from *Situational Factors in Leadership* by John K. Hemphill.

Charles Scribner's Sons for quotations from *Character in Human Relations* by Hugh Hartshorne.

University of Chicago Press for quotations from *Dynamic Groups at Work* by Herbert A. Thelen.

CONTENTS

PART III: The Creative Culture of the Group

FIGURES

Thou wilt light my candle.

—Psalm 18:28

Be ye doers of the word, and not hearers only.

—James 1:22

PART I | *Theory and Mechanics*

1. Using Group Experience to Encourage Spiritual Growth:
THE WORKING CONCEPTS

The face-to-face relationships of people working together on a problem in purposeful, God-related groups provide experiences which contribute to personal maturity, the development of participant skills, and the attainment of spiritual poise. Within every group in every church an untapped reservoir of social energy exists. This potential can be harnessed and put to work to produce change in people and in the world in which they live their lives. Any church can enrich its ministry by giving attention to the principles and practices that mobilize its activities as a group workshop. Out of the face-to-face experiences of men as they associate together in the spirit of Jesus emerges a deeper and clearer insight into life's use and meaning. Once the group workshop is understood and accepted as a way of life, its approaches undergird and strengthen the whole effective mission of the church.

Thinking about the concept of the church as a group workshop can best begin with basic definitions. For purposes of this discussion the church is considered to be the witnessing group of believers at work in the world to make the love and mercy of God living power in their own lives, in the lives of others, and in the social order. The church functions as a group workshop when its program is so planned and administered as to help people to discover and to do worth-while things with increasing participant skill, with a growing sense of the larger significance of their co-operation, and in the spirit of Christian love.

The purpose of the church operated as a group workshop is to produce *change*. Neither the individual nor the world in which he thinks, feels, and acts remains the same after a crea-

3

tive meeting. The concept of change lies at the very core of the dynamic behavior of people in face-to-face groups. Change means the quantity and quality of production resulting from the performance of roles in purposeful groups. The index of this change is reflected in the ease and competence with which a group deals with its problems. Evidences of change appear in the form of more mature participating skills, clearer goals, restructured relationships, new attitudes, the achievement of shared social purposes, the development of more effective technologies, and the shaping of a culture that makes the group more responsive to goal-directed adjustment and more confident in its action. Change may be observed in the accelerated tempo at which the group responsibly approaches and deals with its problems. It may be reflected in the expectations which the participants hold of one another. Change is measured by the outcomes realized in personal, social, and spiritual growth; in the better ways in which a group operates; and in the transformations that take place in the world as a result of the group's performance. Change means forward movement in the achievement of goals. It also means what happens to people in the inner theater of their souls and in their relationships to other people and to God.

At the foundation of the whole teaching of the church, as it relates to positive change, lies the motivating concept of *love*. Actually, love means an inner urge-to-action that leads a person into immediate, personal, and helpful contact with others.[1] Love in an outreaching act of helpfulness of one person toward another. Christian love is this and more. It is an outreaching act of helpfulness, understanding, and forgiving companionship. Its characteristic is unlimited self-giving. It affirms a respect for the worth of the person. Walter Rauschenbusch used to say that whoever treats another as a child of God becomes himself a child of God and learns to know him. Love involves a gratitude for God's goodness. It requires a sense of contrition because of man's own imperfection and inadequacy. The spiritual maturity of a person expresses itself through his skill and capacity to work with and through others in the achievement of goals in this positive Christian spirit of outreaching helpfulness. Henderlite defines the meaning of love operationally by saying that there is nothing either sentimental or artificial about the kind of service required by love. Love calls for tough-mindedness and blood and sweat. . . . We must not make the mistake of thinking that love is easy. . . . Love is of the will, requiring thought and decision. It is not a warm feeling only; it contains an element of calculation. . . . The service demanded by Christian love is always immediate and personal. . . . The demand is for me to act where I am.[2]

Moffatt operationally translates Paul's description of the quality of love when he writes:

Love is very patient, very kind . . . knows no jealousy . . . makes no parade . . . gives itself no airs, is never rude, never selfish, never irritated, never resentful . . . is never glad when others go wrong . . . is gladdened by goodness, always slow to expose, always eager to believe the best, always hopeful, always patient.[3]

Every consideration of the church looked upon as a group workshop takes its point of departure from this working concept of love. The emphasis, however, is always on the qualifying verbal adjective "working."

Love as an attitude toward people is always expressed in the performance of a *role*. It is never abstract; it is always specific. Side by side with the concept of love, therefore, stands the concept of the role. A role is a functioning position occupied by an individual in the working program of a group. It is the job a person has to do in teamwork with others to achieve a goal. It is like a position on a ball team which a baseman must skillfully play to win the game. In the current theory of human relationships the role is the social unit.[4] It is like the key which is slipped into the lock; it opens the door. When people who associate with one another in one of the many meetings within a church come to look upon themselves as human beings performing necessary roles to achieve purposeful goals in the spirit of Christian love, then the group begins to be spiritually productive. It ceases merely to go through routine motions; it begins to move forward in a direction.

Research findings in many different fields of social inquiry support the thesis that from heartfelt purposeful activity a spiritual factor emerges. Human worth is not something that

develops in a vacuum; it is the positive product of the interaction of people at work in solving a problem with full consideration of the realities of the situation. The creative social
act occurs as a co-operative event produced by the interaction
of two or more persons associated as equals in purposeful activity. Participation and communication produce expanding
areas of common good. The social act has religious quality to
the extent that it is performed wholeheartedly with insight into its significance and full commitment to the worth-whileness
of its purpose.

Throughout all the discussion of the church operated as a
group workshop, one concept continually recurs: participant
activity. Professor Gordon Allport, of Harvard University, summarizes the principle by saying:

> When an individual is busily engaged in using his talents,
> understanding his work, and having pleasant relations
> with his fellow-workers, then he is . . . "identified" with
> his job. He likes his work; he is absorbed in it; he is pro-
> ductive. In short, he is industrially active; that is to say,
> he is participant.[5]

What Professor Allport says in substance is this:

First, *the individual must be busily engaged in using his
talents*. This means that he must be occupying a functional
role—doing something that he is fitted to do as his part in the
achievement of a goal.

Second, *he must understand his work*. Persons performing
roles are not just going through motions; they are working together to achieve a purpose. They need to know not only what
to do, but they must understand why they are performing the
task. They are moving on a charted course toward a destina-
tion, not riding in circles on a merry-go-round.

Third, *he must have pleasant relations with his pastor and
his fellow workers.*

Participation means the sharing of responsibilities so that
each person involved feels himself to be a useful and necessary part of the whole activity. He is motivated to do his best
to further the achievement of the group purpose. *Involvement*
means the process by which the experience, skill, and interest

of people are enlisted in a common effort of planning and doing to achieve a common goal. *Give people a chance to put their hearts and efforts as equals together in the doing of something worth-while:* this is the thesis. In technical language Allport's formula reads like this: "Maximize the situations where the individual can participate fully and on terms of equal status on projects of joint concern to him and to his associates."[6]

A spiritually productive group provides for participant activity through the search for and discovery of worth-while purposes and the development and execution of programs to achieve these desired ends. It achieves goals by the functioning of roles. A *goal* is a specific objective which a group sets for itself to achieve as a result of a thorough discussion of its desirability, an appreciation of its costs in effort, time, and money; the desirability of its consequences; and an awareness of the factors of reality that may exist as limiting factors in the performance. The church operated as a group workshop encourages the definition of purposeful goals, the involvement of people in participant roles, and the concern for individual and social change which results from effectual group performance.

Readings

CHRISTIAN BACKGROUNDS

DeWolf, L. Harold, *A Theology of the Living Church.* New York: Harper & Brothers, 1953.

Fosdick, Harry Emerson, *The Three Meanings.* New York: Association Press, 1950; and *The Man from Nazareth.* New York: Pocket Books, Inc., 1953.

Hamilton, Edith, *Spokesmen for God.* New York: W. W. Norton & Company, 1949.

Henderlite, Rachael, *A Call to Faith.* Richmond: John Knox Press, 1955.

Madden, Ward, *Religious Values in Education.* New York: Harper & Brothers, 1951.

Murray, Gilbert, *Liberality and Civilization.* New York: Macmillan Company, 1938.

Niebuhr, Reinhold, *An Interpretation of Christian Ethics.* New York: Harper & Brothers, 1935.

Rall, Harris Franklin, *The Teachings of Jesus.* New York: Abingdon-Cokesbury Press, 1930.

Rauschenbusch, Walter, *The Social Principles of Jesus.* New York: Association Press, 1916.

GROUP ORIENTATION

Brown, J. A. C., *The Social Psychology of Industry*. Hammondsworth: Penguin Books, 1954.

Brown, J. F., *The Psychodynamics of Abnormal Behavior*. New York: McGraw-Hill Book Company, 1940.

Chase, Stuart, *Roads to Agreement*. New York: Harper & Brothers, 1951.

Hoslett, Schuyler Dean, editor, *Human Factors in Management*. New York: Harper & Brothers, 1946.

Jaques Elliott, *The Changing Culture of a Factory*. London: Tavistock Publications, 1951.

Lippitt, Gordon L., and Schmidt, Warren H., *My Group and I* (booklet). Washington, D. C.: Educator's Washington dispatch, DuPont Circle.

Moffatt, James, *Jesus on Love to God; Jesus on Love to Man*. Philadelphia: University of Pennsylvania Press, 1922.

Parsons, Talcott, and Shils, Edward A., editors, *Toward a General Theory of Action*. Cambridge: Harvard University Press, 1951.

Slavson, S. R., *Creative Group Education*. New York: Association Press, 1948.

Sluckin, W., *Minds and Machines*. Hammondsworth: Penguin Books, 1954.

Sorokin, Pitrim A., *Altruistic Love: A Study of American Good Neighbors and Christian Saints*. Boston: Beacon Press, 1950; *Explorations in Altruistic Love and Behavior*, Beacon Press, 1950; *Types, Techniques, and Factors of Altruistic Experiences*, Beacon Press, 1954; and *The Ways and Power of Love*, Beacon Press, 1954.

Sullivan, Dorothea F., *Readings in Group Work*. New York: Association Press, 1952; and *Group Process in Administration*. New York: Woman's Press, 1950.

Trecker, Harleigh B., *How to Work with Groups*. New York: Woman's Press, 1952; and *Social Group Work: Principles and Practices*, Woman's Press, 1948.

2.

Making Groups Productive:

THE EFFECTIVE CLIMATE

Ever since Hugh Hartshorne and Mark May began their research in character education a quarter of a century ago, social
scientists have suspected that moral character is a group phe-
nomenon as well as a personal attribute.[1] So much did Hartshorne believe this thesis that he stated this principle: "Character is a by-product of wholehearted purposeful activity."[2] The
man of character derives joy, confidence, and strength from
successful and meaningful participation in purposeful group
relationships. An effective climate conducive to group productivity does exist. The group is one of the primary power-
houses of moral education. Character has group roots; and the
church which operates as a group workshop deepens these
group roots by strengthening healthy patterns of interpersonal relationships. Hartshorne puts it this way: "The normal
unit for character education is the group or small community
which provides through co-operative discussion and effort the
moral support required for the adventurous discovery and effective use of ideas in the conduct of affairs."[3]

Group experiences that have moral value are not added to
the ordinary activities of life; they consist of those very activities themselves when they are carried on with full realization
of their significance. Thus in the church operated as a group
workshop there are no routine meetings. Every group session
provides an occasion for goal-directed production, personal
growth, and spiritual experience. The meeting stands always
as a great occasion in the ministry of the church.

A meeting which has religious quality is *functional.* Hartshorne defines a function to mean "a helpful act performed glad-

9

ly and efficiently, and with full appreciation of its immediate purpose and its value for the co-operating groups, or for others who are affected, as well as with a sense of fellowship with those who are directly or indirectly involved. . . . Functioning is relational activity."[4] His suggestion deserves careful word analysis. First of all, a function is an act—the doing of something, the performance of a role. Second, this act must be helpful—it must advance the group purpose toward its objective. Third, the helpful act must be performed gladly—the person's heart must be in the doing of the helpful act. Fourth, he must perform the act efficiently—with skill and economy of time, energy, money, and effort. Fifth, the whole helpful act skillfully and sincerely performed must be executed with perspective—with an awareness that it is worth while and with a concern for its consequences. True social functioning exists when each person, performing his specific role in the group, contributes his ideas, his experience, his will, his skill, his strength, and his heart to the enterprise upon which the group is engaged. He shares in the planning. He bears responsibility for the achievement of the common goal.

For purposes of summarizing the factors that operate to deepen the group roots of character, Figure 1 puts together ten identifiable characteristics of group activity which contribute to individual character when studied from the perspective of group membership and action. A group that has character-building value must have ends in view which the group members believe are worth while. These purposes must be useful—they must set up a target which the group members believe is worth hitting. The forward movement toward that target goal must be developed through substantial organization. This means that tasks must be broken down, defined, and co-ordinated; in musical terminology, the instruments must become an ensemble. In any dynamic and creative group the members must possess the skill required to perform each component task as assigned. In every group an in-service training program is always going on to assist the individual to improve his capability for performing his role. Character stutters when skill competence is lacking or skill perfection is not constantly pursued. A pianist who stumbles through the hymns frustrates the whole group and suffers personally because of his inade-

Figure 1.

GROUP ROOTS OF CHARACTER

A group helps to build character when its roles:

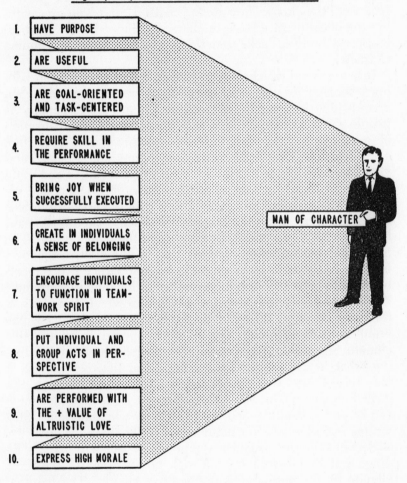

I.	HAVE PURPOSE
2.	ARE USEFUL
3.	ARE GOAL-ORIENTED AND TASK-CENTERED
4.	REQUIRE SKILL IN THE PERFORMANCE
5.	BRING JOY WHEN SUCCESSFULLY EXECUTED
6.	CREATE IN INDIVIDUALS A SENSE OF BELONGING
7.	ENCOURAGE INDIVIDUALS TO FUNCTION IN TEAM-WORK SPIRIT
8.	PUT INDIVIDUAL AND GROUP ACTS IN PER-SPECTIVE
9.	ARE PERFORMED WITH THE + VALUE OF ALTRUISTIC LOVE
10.	EXPRESS HIGH MORALE

MAN OF CHARACTER

quacy. Yes, any group which provides the climate for character growth requires performance skills. Every group needs to recognize this fact and provide for proper training. At an ice-skating party those who cannot skate stand on the sidelines—they are not participant. Indeed they cannot become participant until they know "how to do." Skills, Hartshorne says without qualification, are basic to character. Indeed, "the good intentioned bungler lacks something which belongs to genuine character."[5]

It is a general psychological principle that people enjoy doing what they do well—and increasingly better. Any role when successfully performed gives satisfaction and joy to people. As people share a common idea and work toward the realization of a common goal, they develop *functional craftsmanship.* They feel that they belong together. Something oversize and vital has been created in skillful doing that is larger and more purposeful than the sum of all the individuals associated together. The members are functioning with oneness of purpose as a team. They have the team spirit because each man plays his part with a concept of the purpose of the whole group. The individual performances express the spirit of altruistic love, because each team member seeks to help every other member by the high skill and high quality of his own performance and his goal-directed concern. Any group which functions in this way develops high morale. Its performance deepens the group roots of character. The members operate in an effective climate. Since character develops in groups which are productive, that is, in groups which bring about positive change, it may be said that such groups are healthy. They stimulate the growth of sound Christian selves. Groups, let it be understood, can be just as healthy—and just as sick—as a human being. Sick groups manufacture spiritually sick people.

Fortunately the behavior symptoms of sick groups can be diagnosed by observation. A sick group operates within a climate that is unproductive of positive change. The habitual ways of carrying on activities in a sick group fail to provide for full and genuine exploration, involvement, participation, and action. They do not encourage growth among the broad base of membership. The sick group, recognized from a study of its symptoms, becomes a timid, suspicious, trivial, and ingrown aggregation. It tends to be undemocratic, unresourceful, and afraid of change. It provides no challenges and brings to focus no major issues. Such a group is not only sick; it is moving futilely to slow but certain death. A healthy group, on the other hand, is productive for the very opposite reasons. Its members possess developed participant skill. Communication and participation are full and effectual. When the symptoms of a healthy group are placed side by side with the converse symptoms of the sick group, it becomes obvious from the juxtaposition that the conditions which make for a sick or healthy group are within the control of the group members: they can work toward making their group what they want it to be.

Study for a moment the comparative symptoms of healthy and sick groups:

HEALTHY	SICK
A group is healthy when	A group is sick when
1. all the members speak up about what they think	1. a few members do all the talking
2. decisions are worked through until a general consensus of agreement is reached	2. most members mumble assent
3. well-informed members contribute ideas in the area of their competence	3. competent people sit silently by
4. a member's value is judged by the merit of his idea	4. new people with good ideas are not listened to
5. the whole group handles questions that concern the whole group	5. decision-making is quickly referred to committees
6. major issues get major time	6. minor issues consume the major time
7. major issues evoke mature approaches to change and "working through"	7. minor and simple issues make people seethe and boil
8. minor issues are settled with the attention they deserve	8. major issues are passed over
9. decisions reached by thorough participation are final and satisfactory	9. the same subjects, supposedly settled, keep coming up again
10. members really understand one another's ideas, plans, and proposals	10. quick judgments are passed on issues people do not understand
11. members objectively center interest on goals and tasks	11. members subjectively talk about people in scapegoating
12. the group carries forward in the performance of tasks and the achievement of goals	12. the group accomplishes little in absence of the chairman
13. the group works goalwise toward change	13. the group is afraid of change
14. rewards and criticism are shared	14. rewards and criticism are concentrated in a few

15. initiative and responsibility are encouraged by growth in a sense of personal confidence, competence, and worth	15. initiative and responsibility are stifled by dependence
16. search for help from all sources is continuous	16. no resources outside the group are drawn upon
17. information is fed back into the group	17. little is told to the group
18. the worth of persons is respected	18. the person is squelched in his expression and stunted in his growth
19. experience is considered the occasion for growth in responsibility and love	19. action lacks altitude and depth, remaining on the horizontal plane without vertical relationships to God
20. action is God-related	20. action is self-centered

In the same way that it is possible to study a group to determine whether it is sick or healthy, one can identify the conditions which make for a productive group. A group is productive (1) when it has a clear purpose; (2) when its operations provide freedom for people to contribute their experience and ideas in planning; (3) when members play clearly defined roles in the group structure; (4) when each member bears responsibility for a clearly defined and worth-while task to the performance of which he can devote his imagination, his skill, his initiative, and his heart; (5) when mutual and constructive criticism makes for progress in the achievement of the group's purpose; (6) when skills for working with and through other people strengthen the feeling of personal worth of each; (7) when minds are open to change; (8) when a friendly, responsible, unanxious, participant atmosphere exists; (9) when tasks are performed with confident spirit characterized by wholehearted co-operation, mutual respect, and altruistic love; (10) when people gain personal satisfaction in worth-while achievement through their pooled efforts; (11) when reverence for personality is a guiding ethic; and (12) when the activity is goal-oriented, task-centered, and God-related. A group that gives a satisfying role experience to its members is one that provides "growing space" for people in a "goal-oriented and task-centered program" productive of change which the members feel to be worth while.

A productive group must provide role satisfaction to its members. Members find that role satisfaction only when they operate in situations which demand their mastery of new knowledge and their performance with improved and new skills, and which provide opportunity for practice in the use of a new power. The test of a good moral situation conducive to role satisfaction is the extent to which the task provides people with the opportunity to "try out" the principles. Practice in the skill of doing is essential to every step in character growth and role satisfaction.

Since there is a constant movement of people in and out of groups, it is important for people who work with people to understand the whole cycle of group membership. This cycle may be described in terms of four stages. *Before joining the group* the "sought-after non-member" is unaware that he is a potential recruit; then sees himself as a possible member; and finally visualizes himself in a new role relating his own desires and drives to the aims and structure of the church. *When he does join the group,* the new member becomes involved in a two-way human relationship, asking himself: "What do I expect of this church?" and wondering: "What does this church expect of me?" *Living with the group as an active member,* he continually seeks role satisfaction. He wants activity to make him feel that both he and the church are worth while. He seeks opportunity to grow as a person with increasing skill and competence. Finally, *the ex-member leaves the group;* he withdraws for want of role satisfaction. Sometimes he drops out for reasons which do not reflect on the purposes or program of the group. On the other hand, he may terminate his membership for reasons which the group ought to know for its own good. Under such circumstances a group can well conduct a post mortem to find out the cause of the attrition.

Indeed, every group has a life history. It may experience youth, maturity, old age, and death. The group differs in its life cycles from the individual human being, however, in this characteristic: it possesses within itself the possibility of rejuvenation. By constant change and adaptation it can continue as a vital and mature functioning entity—just so long, let it be understood, as its productivity provides genuine role satisfaction to its members.

What conditions supply this quality of member satisfaction? Fortunately the principles that contribute to member satisfaction can be stated in summary form. A satisfying group:

1. Maintains respect for individual integrity.
2. Emphasizes mutuality of contribution.
3. Avoids making one feel he is "being used" or "taken advantage of."
4. Rotates offices to give all members opportunity to experience roles and exercise initiative.
5. Builds and keeps open channels of communication between all members and those members momentarily in official roles.
6. Evaluates its purposes regularly.
7. Reviews periodically the role performance of members, their participation, and the degree to which the group fulfills member expectations.
8. Has a concern for the total membership cycle by clearly defining what the group stands for and is doing; inducting, orienting, and locating new members in satisfying roles for effective participation; providing opportunities for members to explore new fields of interest which may differ from routine patterns; offering opportunities for emerging leadership so that members can discover new potentialities within themselves; encouraging the progressive development of skills and "know how"; recognizing good performance with sincere appreciation; arranging terminal facilities through which members may conclude their relationship to the group.

When one studies the characteristics of a healthy, role-satisfying, productive group carefully, one finds that these four factors coexist: vision, reality, reverence, and leadership.

By *vision* is meant the intellectual and spiritual faculty which senses a problem worthy to command the interest of the group.

By *reality* is meant the readiness to face conditions which facilitate or limit the solution of a problem to the extent that these conditions are independent of the will of any or all the persons in the group. These conditions may be in the world outside the group. Some of them may exist within the culture and the resources of the group itself. In any case a group that does not act according to policies and programs which reckon with the facts of life moves in a phantom world. Any productive group must take account of the world as it is—its limitations as well as its possibilities.

By *reverence* is meant the recognition of the worth of every man. Every man is different. Each has a different life history, different capabilities; yet each has unique contributions to make to the whole. Jesus did not solve the problem of feeding the five thousand until Andrew recruited the lad who had brought his lunch—five barley loaves and two small fishes. Reverence implies a pattern of performance expectation of members in their functional role. That expectation is that each will feel free and be obliged to contribute his best to help define and achieve the group purpose. Reverence in group action requires mutual encouragement for each to give all to the limits of capacity—like the widow with her mite. Only when such completeness of self-giving exists are miracles performed and change achieved. The panicky Philip discovered this fact to his amazement when he observed the productive power which resulted from the teamwork of Jesus and the boy.

By *leadership*, a subject to be discussed later in detail, is meant the catalytic functional role in a group which accelerates positive change by involving people, keeping open the channels of communication, bringing decision choice-points to focus, and encouraging the development of a consensus of opinion and agreement soundly conceived in the light of full information and an awareness of consequences.

When a group recognizes the real facts, when its members show reverence for the worth of one another, when leadership facilitates participation and growth, the group becomes productive. Such a productive group is goal-oriented, task-centered, and God-related. But how are such goals, roles, and spiritual energy developed? The answers to these questions will be developed in the subsequent chapters of this study. Here let it be only restated that a productive group is one that is confidently performing its purpose with skill, member-satisfaction, and spiritual purpose. Such a group lives and acts with a quality which may be described as "high morale." The total performance of such a group creates a spiritual value that infuses the members with a deep sense of soul-satisfying achievement. The group possesses a buoyant cohesiveness expressive of good health, good work, and good religion. This factor of morale exists as a plus element over and above the skillful performance by each member of his role. It is in truth "a working of the spirit" among people of "one accord."

Readings

Hartshorne, Hugh, *Character in Human Relations*. New York: Charles Scribner's Sons, 1933.

Hartshorne, Hugh, and May, Mark, *Studies in Deceit*. New York: Macmillan Company, 1928; *Studies in Service and Self-Control*, Macmillan Company, 1929; and *Studies in the Organization of Character*, Macmillan Company, 1930.

Murphy, Gardner, *Personality*. New York: Harper & Brothers, 1947.

Thelen, Herbert A., *Dynamics of Groups at Work*. Chicago: University of Chicago Press, 1954, especially pp. 128-217.

3.

Defining Goals to Be Achieved by Purposeful Action:

THE OPERATIONAL MECHANICS

The National Council of Churches in a small manual suggesting goal planning for group action says:

> These words are addressed to you who, with others, are now planning to rethink what your local church is doing. Many local churches have looked squarely at what they are doing, discovered the weak spots, found the causes of failure, reached out to new and needed types of service, and actually strengthened and vastly improved what they were doing. What others have done, this guide has been prepared to help you and your church to do.[1]

In the "thinking and planning" operation directed toward the definition of goals to be achieved by purposeful action, a church deals with the fundamentals of group organization. Members formulate and direct to themselves for answer a series of five searching questions:

1. What should our church do? The answer to this question fixes goals, establishes *policy*, defines a course of action, and sets up targets to be aimed at.
2. How should we accomplish what we decide to do? The answer to this question establishes a *program* of action and a time schedule of work.
3. What tasks need to be performed to execute the program? The answer to this question identifies the *roles* which must be occupied to achieve goals as charted in the program.
4. What people should be involved in the various roles to provide for their own spiritual growth as well as to get

the work done? The answer to this question involves *people* in roles.

5. How will the activity provide experiences to strengthen the religious quality of living? The answer to this question determines the possibilities for *change and growth in the way of Christian love.*

The functional pattern of the "working" group thus involves the co-ordination of policy, program, roles, people, and religious values: clear policy, a definite program of action to achieve the goals set by the policy, a schedule of roles necessary to accomplish the mission, the careful choice of persons to occupy these roles in the task force necessary to accomplish the objective, and the utilization of the experience to change and further spiritual growth. If these points are projected on a worksheet, they look like this:

I	II	III	IV	V
The goals we seek	*Our plan for achieving these goals*	*Tasks necessary to execute this program*	*The right persons matched and assigned to the proper role*	*Change and growth possibilities*
POLICY	PROGRAM	ROLES	PERSONNEL	SPIRITUAL VALUE

Organization Must Be Substantial

The productive group in the workshop church can be no more effective than the soundness of its organizational pattern which mobilizes the energies and aspirations of people to achieve goals. "Take away my mills and factories, but leave me my organization," said Andrew Carnegie, "and I will be back in business." The General Electric Company, which has given profound study to organizational development, says:

A review of the organization history of American businesses which have advanced consistently through the churning economic seas of the past 40 years shows that, fundamentally, their physical growth has come parallel to, but following, a growth toward what you might safely call "managerial maturity." . . . Skillful, creative management has been the necessary forerunner of enduring corporate growth, not only in this dynamic country of ours but on an increasingly world-wide scale.[2]

A church group which fully accepts the responsibility of its mission can be no less concerned with sound organization and management than the General Electric Company.

The fundamental operations involved in group management are four: planning, organizing, integrating, measuring. A productive group is one that is soundly organized. Every group in the workshop church should ask itself a few pointed questions:

PLANNING

Are we directing our energies and resources to the problem which will maximize our contribution?
Have we written out our policy statement?
Have we specified the goals to be achieved by our organized activities?
Have we reckoned with the realities, the factors that limit and facilitate our activities?

ORGANIZING

What steps do we propose to take to achieve our goals?
What roles must be performed?
What skills are necessary for the performance of the roles?
Have we designed an organizational diagram showing how the roles are functionally divided and co-ordinated?
Have we thought through and written out role specifications, job definitions describing the basic function of each job—its scope, its duties, its responsibilities?
Have we provided for instruction and training?
Have we a budget and supply program to support the work and workers with money and equipment?
Have we an operational timetable?

INTEGRATING

Have we provided for communication and participation?
Have we developed ways to facilitate the development of oneness of purpose, of morale?
Have we a plan for continuing effective communication?
Have we a plan for reporting?

MEASURING

Have we a plan for measuring productive change?
Do we know what we want to happen when?
How do we propose to audit the results of our performance?

The continuing and final program audits determine the extent to which outcomes have been achieved in terms of goals projected. The effectiveness of group performance, let it be repeated, depends upon the thoroughness of the organizational pattern and the spiritual consent given to the common goals of effort. It makes no difference whether the operation conducted is a strawberry social put on by the Ladies Aid Society, a conference scheduled by young people, or a canvass planned by the authoritative board to raise funds for a new educational unit and fellowship hall.

Within the church conducted as a group workshop, the program audit of positive change requires answers to questions which override the general achievement. The activity has been conducted, both as an end in itself and as a means to strengthen the religious quality of life. The concern for outcomes of the goal-directed and task-centered activity in the workshop church always raises the question: "What has been the effect of this program on people?" For example:

1. Has the operation provided opportunity for people to grow?
2. Has it provided new content knowledge and widened horizons of life and responsibilities?
3. Has it provided opportunities for people to master and practice new skills?
4. Has it provided opportunities for people to improve participant skills?
5. Has it provided experiences by which people have matured in reverence and the working concept of love?

In short, has the total effect of the program been to bring men closer to God and closer to one another with a depth of meaning and understanding which strengthens life purposes? Has God encountered man in the experiences of the workshop church? All of these questions may be summed up in an omnibus inquiry: Has the group program brought about change as measured by goal achievement; a matured participation skill in the culture of the group; and a greater reverence in the relationships of individuals to man and to God?

In every healthy group there should be a series of work papers. These should include (1) a clear policy statement, (2) an organizational diagram, (3) an operations calendar schedule of the phases to be performed within time limits, (4) job specifications, (5) a plan for enlistment and training, (6) a budget and supply program, (7) a plan for communication, (8) a plan for measuring performance, and (9) an operations manual which describes how the organizational pattern is built, how it works, and how the program is shaped to achieve goals as stated in the policy. The development of these written statements is not burdensome. They are all parts of the "thinking through" phases of sound group management.

Three case histories will illustrate the meaning of "defining policies and building programs."

POLICY MUST RECKON WITH REALITY

An inquiry into a youth program will provide a substantial point of departure for purpose of illustration. Take the following statement of a distinguished judge:

> Having sat in judgment on thousands of defendants in the criminal court, murderers, robbers, rapists, burglars, etc., I have observed that over 85 per cent of the criminals were non-church goers. . . . I have also presided over the Divorce Court for five consecutive years and have commiserated with more than 120,000 litigants over their domestic difficulties and those of their children. Here, too, I have found that same high percentage of non-church goers. J. Edgar Hoover reports even a higher rate. Out of 8,000 delinquent children called to his attention, only 42 attended Sunday School regularly.[3]

A simple deduction from this statement is that people who go to church do not get in trouble with the law. Hence the problem of delinquency and divorce might be solved by increased church attendance! How? Certainly not by the multiplication of platitudes! Certainly not by reiteration of social woes! Here is a problem worthy of the best efforts of the Christian Church. But the best-motivated Christians soon collide with the facts of reality. If one reckons with reality, he discovers that the delinquents as a group are distinguished from the non-delinquents:

(1) *physically*, in being essentially mesomorphic in constitution (solid, closely knit, muscular);

(2) *temperamentally*, in being restlessly energetic, impul-

sive, extraverted, aggressive, destructive (often sa-
distic)—traits which may be related more or less to
the erratic growth pattern and its physiologic cor-
relative or consequences;

(3) *in attitude,* by being hostile, defiant, resentful, suspicious, stubborn, socially assertive, adventurous, un-
emotional, non-submissive to authority;

(4) *psychologically,* in tendency to be direct and concrete, rather than symbolic, intellectually expressive,
and in being less methodical in their approach to
problems;

(5) *socioculturally,* in having been reared to a far greater
extent than the control group in homes of little understanding, affection, stability, or moral fibre by
parents usually unfit to be effective guides and protection or, according to the psychoanalytic theory, desirable sources for emulation and the construction of
a consistent, well-balanced, and socially normal su-
perego during the early stages of character development.[4]

It is obvious that no traditional church program is designed to
meet the needs of youth answering to these specifications. How
can a policy and a program be developed to provide opportunities for growth in satisfying roles of boys and girls answering these specifications?

Upon his graduation from Princeton Theological Seminary
in 1947, Robert Meyer decided to reckon with reality and find
out. Deliberately he accepted a call to a parish covering the
area known as "The Block" in Baltimore, Maryland. "The Block"
as a human environment was a sordid section of a great American city. Sociologists described it as one of the most vicious
and lawless areas in the world. Meyer's physical headquarters,
McKim Center and the Church of the Savior, organizationally
ineffectual institutions, were famous architecturally and historically. In design his headquarters building was an exact
replica of the temple of Theseus in Athens. People who knew
classified it as the purest example of Doric architecture in
America.

Dispensing with the usual tea and reception customarily
provided for the welcome of a new pastor, Meyer proceeded
to "reckon with reality." Disguising himself as a bum, he slept

in the flophouses on the Baltimore waterfront. He observed adolescent girls initiating their careers as prostitutes. He watched boys soliciting for their own mothers and sisters. He met street gangs of both sexes which prowled the streets. He came to know their weapons: knives, brass knuckles, guns, and daggers. He watched the latchkey kids roaming the streets. At first hand he witnessed the intense hatreds, fears, and suspicions of the young people. He experienced a type of human being he had not met within the ivied Princeton walls in the Gothic New Jersey town. Here was youth—hostile, defiant, resentful, and powerful. Vice on "The Block" was a way of life. Thieves, truants, pimps, prostitutes, arsonists, rapists, and muggers were the "professional" and respected class among Meyer's new neighbors.

The life patterns on "The Block," however, were only one phase of the reality with which Meyer had to reckon. True, the church was surrounded by human beings who needed its ministry; that church had members who had no lines of communication with the neighborhood people and no developed skills for dealing with their needs. The *culture* of the church, that is, its usual way of operating, and its *technology*, that is, the set of principles and practices used to carry out its program and achieve its goals, were completely unrelated to the situation. They dealt with a nonexistent world. In the language of semantics, the church was operating according to a map, a picture of the world, which is no way described the territory, the real world. Meyer had to develop policies to accelerate positive change—inside as well as outside the church.

Reckoning with "reality," Meyer began to define goals to be achieved by appropriate and purposeful action. He had no homogeneous group which could sit down and discuss; his "members-to-be" were "out there on the street." All he could do was to experiment with a policy-program, and then develop his dynamic workshop group. He began to ask the basic questions:

1. *What should our church do?*

Policy statement: McKim Center and the Church of the Savior will provide a redemptive Christian ministry designed to meet the needs of youth living on "The Block."

2. *How shall we accomplish what we decide to do?*

Program statement: The policy shall be carried out through a program based on (a) Christian example; (b) friendship; (c) emotional satisfactions more satisfying than the thrills in the folkways of delinquency; (d) love.

3. *What tasks need to be performed to execute the program?*

Meyer inventoried the new roles required to demonstrate that McKim Center provided more adventure and thrills than the underworld life on "The Block." With his boys he shot the Potomac River rapids in a canoe. They sailed Chesapeake Bay in a 40-mile gale. They boxed and wrestled. They played basketball before crowds in the Coliseum. They performed before television cameras. In the center of the program stood the Meyer home. Into it Meyer and his wife invited as their own foster sons eight hard-core problem boys at a time. They reared the lads as their own until they came to peace with their associates, with themselves, and with God.

Meyer demonstrated the final performance of Christian love. He regularly appeared in court when the boys were arraigned. As he sat one morning on the public bench, Meyer saw a boy brought before the court. His record was complete. At eight this lad had been a truant. At nine he was arrested as a shop lifter. At ten he was charged with fifteen robberies. At twelve, in a fit of hate, he had attempted to kill a schoolteacher with a chair. His mother was a prostitute. From the cradle he had faced a world with any word or weapon at hand. At Meyer's request the boy was released in his custody. Haughty and defiant, the boy felt that he had scored against the police once more: he had won another battle against society! Was he not free in the care of a minister?

At McKim Center this boy began to experience new adventures. He met other boys from his gang. Together, under McKim auspices, they started on a 1,500-mile trip to Canada in an old truck. The boys swam at midnight in the bay. They hunted with their rifles. They canoed. They hiked. They camped.

But the therapy was not sufficient. The constant demonstration of Meyer and his wife that clean or dirty, friendly or ugly, good or bad, the boy was always wanted—always loved—seemed to fail. The boy was arrested for stealing. Once again he was released in Meyer's custody and moved into the manse with the Meyers. He was still savage and hostile as he worked out his hate. His efforts culminated in a bedroom battle—he knifed a sixteen-year-old boy. Himself strangled in the affair, he fled into the night when he regained consciousness. Meyer followed the boy out into the darkness. He found the lad and brought him home. Months later the boy said: "You wanted me back!" Persistent love had won its reward. Within two years the boy stood first in his high school class. He joined the Church of the Savior on profession of faith. At sixteen, as he was ready to leave the Meyer home, he gave Meyer a box. "Keep this," he said. "I won't need it any more." Inside was a deadly "zip gun" he had clandestinely manufactured to provide for his security. "The surrender of his gun," Meyer explained, "was the surrender of the old life and the beginning of a new one."

On "The Block" in Baltimore Meyer implemented a policy with a program that reckoned with reality. His work developed a "culture" and a "technology." The situation was one in which Meyer had to recruit a group before he could facilitate its operation as a productive team. It is in the necessity of a missionary mode of action to penetrate areas of need as a precondition of service. Meyer served as an "agent" to catalyze change—inside the neighborhood and inside the church. Henderlite appropriately says:

> The message of the church requires action. God himself chose deeds as a means of revelation. . . . Love cannot be understood so long as it remains a word. Love has to be experienced in order to be known.[5]

PROGRAM MUST PROVIDE ROLE SATISFACTION

Another case history of a quite different order will show how a policy implemented through a program provides role satisfaction. The First Presbyterian Church, Oklahoma City, faced reality and asked a question: "How can we encourage worshipful response of people to God through music?" In the exploratory group discussions it was recalled that Martin Luther wrote hymns for his people so that the whole congregation could respond to the reading of God's word by singing his praise. The power of music "sung to" or "sung for" people never equals the power of music "sung by" people. The session felt that "a singing congregation is a spiritually prayerful church." Henderlite puts it this way:

> When we surrender to God in praise, there comes to us a new and needed perspective in life. We see things in their proper relationship. We recognize ourselves as created ones. We not only accept our creaturehood but we rejoice in the Creator. . . . This is the highest and truest activity of man and is therefore a mark of wholeness.[6]

The First Church policy on music was thus defined to be the development of congregation-wide reverent participation through music. As discussion continued about the nature of the program needed to implement this policy, it became the consensus that a functional ministry of music organized groupwise through a system of graded choirs should provide a choral program for every age and interest. As outlined in Figure 2, the program of participation is planned to begin at birth and continues through all the life cycles.

The church called to the leadership of the program John S. C. Kemp and his wife, Helen Kemp, as ministers of music. With the music committee the Kemps spelled out a policy and a program. Upon adoption this was printed for church-wide distribution as an eight-page leaflet.[7]

In a period of five years the church developed its pattern of graded choirs to involve more than six hundred boys and girls and men and women a year. In addition to these members of choral groups, there are roles for nearly a hundred others who serve as choir mothers, choir daddies, and workers on the "logistics" staff. The goal of all is the development of mature habits of worship on the part of all the people through the instrumentality of music.

The various choral groups are used as vehicles for experience in developing the attitude of "understanding helpfulness." During a work session, for example, the Kemps will call "time out" to work with individual boys and girls. During such periods choir members show two characteristic attitudes. The first attitude is expressed by the individual who is being helped: he does his best to overcome his difficulty and to meet the members of the whole group on a new level of competence. On its part the group as a whole listens attentively: it tries to help those who are being given special coaching. There is no laughter when some boy or girl gets off pitch. As one lad observed: "If anybody laughs, nobody can be helped." Each boy and girl grasps the attitude: "I'm here to help. It's my responsibility."

The choral program for the young people is closely integrated with the Youth Club schedule, as can be seen from the following chart:

SCHEDULE FOR YOUTH CLUB AND WEDNESDAY PROGRAM

	4:00	4:45	5:30	6:05	7:00
K-1	Carol Choir	Recreation	Supper	Story Time and Creative	
2-3	Jr. Ch. Choir	Recreation	Supper	Bible Activities	
4-5-6	Bible Study	Chapel Choir	Supper	Recreation	Library
7-8-9	———	Descanters Chanticleers	Bible Study	Supper	and Crafts
10-11-12	———	———	Bible Study	Supper	H. S. Choir
Y. Adults	———	———	———	Supper	Bible Study
Adults	———	———	———	Supper	Bible Study

The choir program is family-centered as well as church-centered. The whole church takes a "hymn of the month." For four consecutive Sundays all the people join in the study and singing of that one hymn. Whole families memorize stanzas. They practice them at home, sing them together around the family piano, and on Sundays in the family pew sing them without hymnals.

Reaching further into the family life, the choral program encourages the boys and girls to sing the blessing at the family table. To the tune of Bach's chorale "Jesus, Joy of Man's Desiring," the children sing the words of the old German grace:

> *Jesus, be our guest today;*
> *Bless this food, dear Lord, we pray. Amen.*

Each choral group has its own special occasion for singing, but all groups have the same single purpose: response to God in worship by singing praises to him. The technologies developed for the various groups are tailor-made to age-group needs. As soon as a child is born, people of the church visit the mother

Figure 2.

SYSTEM OF GRADED CHOIRS
A GROUP FOR EVERY AGE AND INTEREST

FIRST PRESBYTERIAN CHURCH
Oklahoma City, Oklahoma

AGE GROUP	NAME	FUNCTIONAL ACTIVITY GOAL
Babies 1 day to 3 years	THE CRIER CHOIR	Each baby of a church family is automatically enrolled as a "Crier". Occasional parties---no regular rehearsals. Purpose: to enroll all children in the interest of the church and the music program; to communicate the idea that music is natural and fun; to encourage families to think of music as a way of saying things; and to build the foundation for the "choir habit" for children and parents.
3 and 4 year olds	CHERUB CHOIR	Pre-school children--- $2\frac{1}{2}$ hour sessions on Tuesdays during Women's Association and Circle meetings. Purpose: further to develop the choir habit through group response in singing games, singing graces, playing church, and activities.
Kindergarten and 1st grade children	CAROL CHOIR	Most important of all children's groups---rehearsals Mondays at 4:00 o'clock. Purpose: to serve as a "trainer choir"; to sing once a month in Junior Church and on special occasions in Adult Church.
2nd & 3rd grades Primary Division 4th through 6th grades Junior Division	CHAPEL CHOIR	Two groups rehearse separately, but usually perform together---rehearsals Wednesday afternoon in conjunction with Youth Choir. Purpose: to sing every month in adult church on children's baptism Sunday; to perform on special seasonal occasions.
2nd through 6th grades	CHAPEL SINGERS	Junior church choir selected from members of chapel choirs with membership changed periodically. Purpose: responsibility for Junior Church in same way as Sanctuary Singers for adult church.
7th and 8th grade, Girls	DESCANTERS	Rehearses Wednesday afternoon in the Youth Club. Purpose: to sing descants to the hymns in adult worship; to appear as a solo group at meetings and services.
7th and 8th grade, Boys	CHANTICLEERS	Choral reading group rehearses Wednesday afternoon in Youth Club. Purpose: occasionally to read the Sunday morning Scripture; to perform at other meetings; to sing in combined groups.

SYSTEM OF GRADED CHOIRS

(CONTINUED)

AGE GROUP	NAME	FUNCTIONAL ACTIVITY GOAL
9th through 12th grades	HIGH SCHOOL CHOIR	Performing choir of sixty members—-rehearse Wednesday 8:00 to 9:00 p.m. Purpose: to give special concerts at neighboring churches; occasionally to replace the Sanctuary Singers in the morning worship; to sing at vesper services.
College men and women	COLLEGIATE CHOIR	Performing choir--- rehearse Thursday nights during the summer at 7:45 o'clock. Purpose: to perform at morning worship services during the summer months--- June, July, and August.
Adults	SANCTUARY SINGERS	Performing choir of eighty---rehearse Thursday 7:45 p.m. Purpose: to lead in each Sunday morning worship service; to make worship a deep Christian experience through music; to do special programs including oratorios and A Cappella concerts.
Men	MEN'S CLUB CHORUS	Choir for all male voices. Purpose: to provide opportunity for men unable to participate in the regular choir; to provide stimulating companionship in choral work; to make possible "rousing singing" in the Men's Club; to appear occasionally in the regular services.
All ages	INSTRUMENTAL CHOIR	Orchestra. Rehearses 9:00 o'clock Sunday morning. Purpose: to provide music during the summer months and on special occasions.
All ages	AUDIENCE PARTICIPATION	Annual performance of Handel's "Messiah"---rehearses one hour before performance. Purpose: to provide an occasion for all who love to sing to join together in common music fest.

in the hospital to induct the baby into the Crier Choir. They present a certificate, shown in Figure 3, and explain that

> The Crier Choir of the First Presbyterian Church is composed of talented vocalizers between the ages of one day and three years. The only requirement for membership is conscientious and diligent vocal exercise. Inasmuch as the members of this choir sing in many keys, in diverse ranges, with divided emotions and with varying degrees of intensity, it has been deemed advisable to dispense with the usual choir rehearsal. As a substitute, one or two parties based on varying themes will be given each year. Parents will be notified when such parties are held.

The High School Choir assumes a responsibility for working with youth groups in outlying communities. Its members help to organize choirs, join in common song fests and youth programs, hold occasional seminars and song clinics, and engage in social functions.

One of the important parts of the program which increases role satisfaction is the carefully organized training program. Individual and group lessons are provided for the choir members. Each fall program is initiated by a week-long training and leadership workshop. Young people who show special promise of leadership are sent to a series of summer camps and schools, including the Westminster Choir School at Princeton, New Jersey.

By means of a carefully built program designed to carry out a clearly defined policy with deep group roots, the First Presbyterian Church has developed a worship program which encourages personal, spiritual, and aesthetic growth. The church has become a great singing congregation.

POLICY AND PROGRAM MUST BE ORGANICALLY INCORPORATED INTO CHURCH ORGANIZATIONAL PATTERN

Policies and programs of workshop groups must be organically incorporated into the organizational structure of the church. The workshop group must never be a sideshow. Idlewild Presbyterian Church, Memphis, Tennessee, demonstrates an effective organizational pattern in its recreational program.

The general philosophy of the place of recreation in the

Figure 3.   **CRIER CHOIR MEMBERSHIP CERTIFICATE**

church program can perhaps best be explained by these statements:

> It is good for a man to be able at times to just enjoy being alive, good for him to meet with his fellows free from obligations to study anything in particular. . . . Out of such fellowships come a gladness and a joy that stimulate one to renewed interest in living.[8]

> The highest relationship possible between persons is that of mutual enjoyment. The natural enjoyment of God is worship. The enjoyment of man and nature is play. Both are goals or ends of the Christian life. True worship can come only when we have made our peace with God and grown up into fellowship with Him; real play can occur only when both we and the brother have been released from our slavery to ourselves and brought into fellowship with one another. . . . Play is marked by respect for personality or more truly by appreciation for personality. There is a disinterestedness or objectivity in play life like the disinterestedness in worship. When we are engaged in play, we are not primarily self-centered. We enjoy the companionship of the other and provide enjoyment for the other. . . . In play we are not seeking profit of any kind; we play for the sheer joy of playing. There is nothing risked, nothing at stake, nothing to be gained. We are not working now to lift the status of the brother; we are enjoying him as he is. We play with another to match wits with him, for the fun of matching wits—he will win this time and I the next. We play with one another because we enjoy his companionship and he enjoys ours. . . . That play is one of the exalting and regenerating experiences in the life of human beings is a truth that we have been slow to include among our Christian beliefs. We have approached play with divided minds. We have often played with guilty consciences, enjoying it but feeling that we should not. . . . We have seldom understood play as a natural expression of a soul at one with God and man. . . . The simple happiness that marked the life of Jesus makes any other interpretation forever impossible. . . . Play cannot be thought of as the way to life or the way to avoid life, but it must be thought of as a natural accompaniment of life with Christ, when all of our capacities are heightened, and life is given a new dimension. . . . The freedom and

grace that come to us as "gifts of the Spirit" may well express themselves in play—in this joyous outpouring of the self in companionship with the brother, whom we love as we love ourselves, and whom we enjoy not for our own sakes alone but for his sake and for Christ's sake.[9]

With twenty-five hundred members, Idlewild Presbyterian Church recognizes the place which play holds in the ministry of the church. In the development of its extensive ministry of recreation, Idlewild has learned a good deal about the kind of organizational pattern which supports effective program work. Its experience shows clearly that an activity of the church functioning as a group workshop must have deep roots in the organic structure of the congregation. The experience of Idlewild can perhaps best be shared by a statement and explanation of basic principles on which it has developed its programs:

Principle 1. *The recreation program should be organized through a strong committee responsible to the governing board of the church.* This means that the membership on the recreation committee should include outstanding individuals in the church and the community whose decisions carry weight. This committee concerns itself with the scope, vitality, and service of the program. At Idlewild the committee reports directly to the session.

Principle 2. *The work of the committee on recreation should be subdivided into task units dealing with functional areas such as athletics, arts and crafts, homemaking skills, dramatics, social activities, senior citizens, and camping.* This means that each functional area should have the specialized thinking and skilled leadership of qualified persons deeply concerned with the field. At Idlewild, over eighty adults are involved in the planning and production of the recreation program.

Principle 3. *The leadership skills required to carry out the program should be inventoried, and qualified people should be found to occupy the roles.* This means that the recreation activity will be supported by a sound personnel program.

Principle 4. *Recreation programs should be introduced only as qualified volunteers are available and only when adequate facilities have been developed.* This means that a church can only discharge its responsibility in the ministry of recreation when it has the equipment and personnel for doing the job well. A church which bungles into recreational activities is walking on thin ice.

PRINCIPLE 5. *Indoor and outdoor programs should be developed to meet the needs of all interest and age groups.* This means that a church recreation program does not need to be confined to the physical church property. Likewise it means that the church grounds are areas to be developed, quite as much as basements.

PRINCIPLE 6. *The budget for the support of the recreation program should be included in the regular current expense budget of the church.* This means that the recreation program should not be "something extra" but an organic part of the whole church ministry.

PRINCIPLE 7. *A good recreation program should look forward to full-time and part-time professional recreation leadership.* This means that recreation requires the same kind of specialized professional staff as the ministry of music.

PRINCIPLE 8. *The recreation program of the church should be identified as a part of the whole recreation movement through active membership in the National Recreation Association.* This means that the recreation program of the church is not merely a local activity but a segment of the whole movement in American life.

PRINCIPLE 9. *Leadership recreation workshops should be planned with the co-operation of the National Recreation Association.* This means that a church must plan systematically for the training and retraining of its leaders.

Within the structure of this sound organizational pattern, Idlewild offers a comprehensive recreation program. The recreation building of the church includes among other facilities an attractive lounge with television, books, and magazines; office space for administration and staff; handicraft rooms; a large party room with a snack bar; an equipment room; game rooms with ping-pong tables, skittles, box hockey, scramball, and numerous table games; a sewing room; a model railroad room; boy and girl scout rooms; a cub scout den; and a dark room. The outdoor area provides space for baseball; handball; horseshoes; swings; see-saws; badminton; croquet; volley ball; and other outdoor activities. Organized athletic groups range from baseball, basketball, and touch football to bowling, roller skating, archery, and riflery. Provision is made for roller skating, square dancing, and regular informal and open-house activities for various age groups.

The full program further includes study groups on great books, world affairs, and great music; book reviews; hobby groups concerned with model railroads, photography, woodworking, and numerous handcrafts. It provides occasional short courses in such activities as corsage making, lampshade painting, remodeling old hats, cooking, sewing, and ship modeling. A dramatics group produces plays. There is a weekly morning group in conversational French and Spanish. In short, the recreational programs are planned according to the needs and responses of the church membership by interest groups. Much of the success at Idlewild depends on the voluntary assistance of committees and individuals who realize that their leadership provides a service for the families of the community, including their own.

Other churches approach the recreation ministry in equally substantial ways. The Highland Presbyterian Church, Fayetteville, North Carolina, for example, has a "seven-day-a-week" schedule. There is much experimentation in the adaptation of the program to the needs of the church groups. Highland substitutes a weekday camp for the traditional type of vacation Bible school, which confines children to a building. The day-camp program is developed on a departmental basis, each age group having a full daily schedule of worship, play, handcrafts, music, swimming, and study. Provision for concentration upon one group at a time enables the minister of music and Christian education to spend more time with each child. A local park and lake are utilized in the summer camp program. Highland also provides a functional library service. A garden hobby club assumes the responsibility for beautifying the church grounds, setting out living Christmas trees, and providing a picnic ground for outside church activity.

In the Green Mountains, J. Wesley Hughes developed the idea of the hymn festival from the Welsh *Gymanfa Ganu*. From the library steps on the Wells, Vermont, village green, a whole community sings. The idea has spread to other towns. The Berkshire Chapter, American Guild of Organists, with ten churches co-operating, brings the year's work of nearly five hundred junior and junior high school choir boys and girls to a climax in Pittsfield, Massachusetts, with a joint presentation directed by a guest conductor and special organist.

Adelle Carlson, of the First Baptist Church, Anderson, South Carolina, says that "recreation in the church is not a part in itself, but is a part of the whole." She divides the phases of church recreation into physical activities; mental activities, such as library and educational programs; creative activities, such as crafts, dramatics, and music; social activities.

In Fairfield, Vermont, Father Francis Candon, pastor of the Roman Catholic Church, takes as a working theory this principle: "Get the parish people to play together, then they'll work together." Putting on overalls, he joined with the nun appointed to the church, and together they worked to provide for recreation through a parish hall, a roomy auditorium, a stage with good footlights, a dance floor, a well-equipped kitchen, and a social hall. They provide programs which include square dances, local talent shows, sleigh rides, skating groups, picnics, and sugaring-off parties. The church provides for what Father Candon calls "friendly fellowship," a center where young people have a chance to meet one another. The recreation facilities at Fairfield exude housekeeping pride. Gay checked covers go on the tables and colorful drapes hang from the windows. Walls are painted in pastel shades. As one observer remarked: "Somebody lives here and cares about things, somebody who really believes the Lord is in the church, and wants his people about him."

A church which develops a recreational program provides goals and roles for people, with opportunity for rewarding activity directed toward the enjoyment and growth of all age and interest groups. A workshop church thoroughly organizes agreed-upon goals, through effective action programs, to provide for participation leading to growth in knowledge, skill, and spiritual poise. Such a program, recognizing reality, providing role satisfaction, and adequately organizing its activities into the structure of the church, brings spiritual joy to people.

Readings

Eisenberg, Helen and Larry, *How to Lead Group Singing*. New York: Association Press, 1955; and *How to Help Folks Have Fun*, Association Press, 1954.

Finegan, Jack, *Youth Asks About Religion*. New York: Association Press, 1949.

Glueck, Sheldon and Eleanor, *Unraveling Juvenile Delinquency*. Cambridge: Harvard University Press, 1955.

Kemp, John S. C. and Helen H., *The Ministry of Music*. Oklahoma City: First Presbyterian Church. Booklet free on request.

Kettering, Don, *Steps Toward a Singing Church*. Philadelphia: Westminster Press, 1948.

National Recreation Association, *Recreation and the Church*. New York: National Recreation Association, 1951; *Recreation Activities for Adults*. New York: Association Press, 1950; and *Recreation for the Aging*, by Arthur M. Williams, Association Press, 1953.

Porter, Joseph P., *Beautifying the Church Grounds*. New York: Interdenominational Bureau of Church Architecture. Ten cents.

Recreation, monthly magazine published by the National Recreation Association, 8 W. 8th St., New York 11, N. Y.

Riggs, Decatur, *How to Use a Parish House*. New York: Bureau of Church Building. Five cents.

Ross, Murray G., *Religious Beliefs of Youth*. New York: Association Press, 1950.

Taylor, Walter A., *Requirements of Drama and Pageantry in the Church*. New York: National Council of Churches. Five cents.

What a Seven-Day-a-Week Church Does. New York: National Council of Churches. Three cents.

Wittenburg, Rudolph M., *So You Want to Help People*. New York: Association Press, 1947; and *On Call for Youth*, Association Press, 1955.

Your Church Library. Chicago: National Council of Churches. Twenty-five cents.

4.

Formulating and Subdividing
Problems into Task Missions:

THE ANALYSIS INTO WORK UNITS

A problem is a question proposed for solution: efforts to work it through to develop the answer provide the meeting point of the individual and the social order. Change results in the process of problem-solving group work, because it is only by experience in exploring and solving problems that human beings learn together. The problem brought sharply to focus provides the teaching situation that initiates learning. In the workshop church it is the face-to-face group exploring and solving problems which becomes the productive instrumentality of positive change. The problem becomes the central axis around which the whole dynamic group functioning revolves.

The amazing thing about the *problem-center* of the workshop group activity is that when the major question is brought sharply to focus, it subdivides and begets a whole series of subsidiary problems that must be solved as a condition for dealing properly with that major question which stands as the focus of group concern. The initial problem-centered group leads to the creation of subordinate problem-centered groups, as Figure 4 shows. These "progeny-problems" call for sub-task forces which can study them and report. Thus the exploration of the original problem identifies *opportunities for depth participation* in the pursuit of the subordinate question. Such activity produces a broad base of specialized competence in the various phases of the total problem. Huszar calls the problem-centered group and subgroups the apparatus of "do democracy": people participate in the common action to face problems together.

Figure 4.

PROBLEM-CENTERED GROUP
BEGETTING OTHER TASK FORCE PROGENY

THE PROBLEM: BIBLE READING

To demonstrate the nature of problem-formulation and problem-subdivision requiring assignment of task forces in the workshop, this chapter will take a statement by Bishop Angus Dun to the effect that

> The Bible can be read religiously, with the eyes of faith. Then we shall come to it seeking answers to the ultimate questions of life. What is man? Who am I? Has life any meaning? Is there anything that does not pass away? What is the greatest treasure? What is the nature of the power with which I must finally reckon? . . . Any discerning reader will quickly realize that the chief character in this great book is God. . . . And happy is the reader who can come to say "Here my God is speaking to me of himself and of me and my neighbors and my world."[1]

On the basis of this paragraph the question is asked: "How indeed can the Bible be read religiously with the eyes of faith?" In formulating this question there are three underlying assumptions: that regular personal Bible reading contributes to a robust and literate Christian life; that "getting the Bible read" exists as one of the chief problems and one of the chief victories of the church; and that Bible reading, being more a matter of habit than impulse, needs systematic cultivation.

Since its organization in 1816 the American Bible Society alone has distributed enough copies of the Scriptures so that every family on earth could have access to one. The whole or parts of the Bible have been published in over six hundred languages. Some thousand languages or dialects remain into which some parts of the Scriptures should still be translated and published. Despite this enormous activity in distribution, people read the Bible little. The American Bible Society says:

> The widespread ignorance of the Bible dismays all serious persons. Many recognize that a certain authority attaches to it, but even to them it is an unknown book. If it ever was important that the Christian forces of America mobilize themselves for effective Bible reading, that time is now. It has been somewhat of a surprise, however, to discover that, while there are countless books on Bible study, on sermon preparation, on religious education, and

definite instruction in every denomination on administrative practices, ordinances, and other phases of the work
of the ministry, there seems to be no collected body of
varied and tested experience by which the pastor and the
church worker can develop a vital attachment to the Bible
as a constant factor in the program of the local church.
When we view the lamentable ignorance of the Bible in
the churches of today, it is difficult to defend the adequacy of any of the current methods.[2]

The American Bible Society conducted a survey to find what
deters people from reading the Bible. It reported its findings:
(1) indifference, (2) worldliness, and (3) carelessness which
afflicts otherwise good people. On the basis of a study of the
religious beliefs of youth, conducted among constituents of the
YMCA, Murray Ross says that in not more than one out of five
cases studied was an integrative religious sentiment at work
in the lives of the youth. Less than that number have what
appears to be any "meaningful communication with God." Perhaps this YMCA study is the most valuable index available on
Bible reading habits. The study showed that during a six-month
period almost four out of five of youth constituents of YMCA's
did not read the Bible at all or read it only "once or twice."
Extremely few of the youths reported that they met with family groups for worship or sat at meals at which grace is said.
"Bible reading, family worship, and grace at meals," said the
report, "are historic religious practices which, to judge by this
group, are fast disappearing."[3]
. The problem becomes clear. Christian people do not read
the Bible as they should. Habits of Bible reading developed in
other days are weakening. The church needs to face head-on
the task of achieving more and more spiritually significant
Bible reading. Any study of the church population will verify
the appalling lack of Bible reading. Action in the Centreville
Community Church on the problem began with a discussion of
a small group convened by the Church Council to prepare an
exploratory report. The *functionally appointed task force* included seven members: the pastor; the proprietor of a local
bookstore; the circulation manager of the local newspaper,
himself a representative young married adult with three children in the church school; the principal of the local high

school; a representative designated by the church committee on evangelism; a representative designated by the church school board; and a competent secretary with the ability to follow up and follow through.

After much study and discussion, the committee suggested a policy: the development of a program, extending over a period of eight weeks, to encourage the reading of the Bible, to clarify the fundamental concepts of the Christian faith, and to relate these concepts to everyday living—the whole purpose being to improve man's communication with God and to make fellowship with him more complete. The Council approved the report and instructed the same committee to proceed with the development of a program in detail and to report back.

Problem Subdivision

The committee had originally suggested an eight-week program. But what eight weeks? Here was a sub-problem which required the study of a special task force. This subcommittee recommended a calendar of dates, beginning with Epiphany on January 6 and extending through March 3. The program was to run into Lent. The time schedule was so planned as to recognize the drama of the Christian year from Advent toward Easter, and looking toward Pentecost. This calendar became the group's basic worksheet.

How should the reading program be designed to clarify certain basic Christian concepts? Here was another sub-question. Then the group faced the question of what Bible should be used as a reading text. The committee knew that every church family was well supplied with a miscellaneous assortment of Bibles, Testaments, and devotional books. Here was another sub-question requiring subcommittee study. After serious evaluation of the pros and cons of using one Bible in preference to another, the subcommittee recommended the use of a paperbound edition of the King James text edited and arranged by James Reeves as *The Holy Bible in Brief* and published as a Mentor Book by the New American Library of World Literature, 501 Madison Avenue, New York 22, at 50 cents. The subcommittee gave a number of reasons for the selection of this book. It is issued in a handy format that can be slipped in the pocket, fitted in the handbag, or held conveniently for easy reading. The paper is good, the type large and strong, and the arrangement of materials such that the whole text can be read at the rate of six pages a day over a period of fifty days. The text is arranged without verse citation, so that the chapter and paragraph structure looks like an ordinary book. The edition is broken down into four books and seventy-five chapters. The division into books follows a useful sequence: Book I—The Story of the Hebrew People; Book II—Hebrew Literature; Book III—Jesus of Nazareth; and Book IV—The Early Christian Church.

Once the committee had decided on the desirability of this edition for the purposes of the eight-week program, it faced the problem of finance. Who would pay for the Bibles? The committee intended to give one copy of the edition to each member of every family in the church. The sum needed for the supply exceeded $500. Here was a special problem of finance; a problem-centered subcommittee was appointed to report on the subject.

But how was this Bible to be distributed? Another subcommittee recommended that the distribution should be made by house-to-house visits when the whole family circle was present. At this time the church reading program would be explained, each person given his copy to write his name in, and a general review of the book given.

The distribution might be effectively accomplished, but how could people be stimulated to read it? Motivating communication? How should the idea be transmitted with power? The whole committee began to enumerate channels of communication:

1. The pastor's sermons
2. The parish newsletter
3. The Sunday church bulletin
4. The church school classes and organized groups in the church
5. Special letters
6. House-to-house visitation
7. Cottage meetings by zones and blocks
8. Bulletin boards and color posters
9. Special leaflets

10. Booklets on the history of the English Bible
11. Slide films
12. Motion pictures
13. Family Bible game
14. Visual slide
15. Quiz sessions

From this preliminary inventory of available communication channels, it became evident that there was need for a special task force to deal with communication—methods of "getting the idea to take."

The committee next decided to explore methods which historically had exercised a positive influence on devotional life. At this point the members concerned themselves with *resource input*. Because method was related to the word "Methodist," the committee set out to discover effective ways which John Wesley used in reading the Scriptures when he was an Oxford student. A subcommittee took the assignment and reported. that often Wesley took a passage from the Bible and paraphrased it in his own words in prose and poetry. He took for example Psalm 104 which reads:

> *Bless the Lord, O my soul.*
> *O Lord my God, thou art very great;*
> *Thou art clothed with honour and majesty.*

Wesley put the words into verse like this:

> *Upborne aloft on vent'rous wings,*
> *While, spurning earthly things,*
> *I soar,*
> *Through paths untrod before,*
> *What God, what seraph shall I sing?*

All agreed that Wesley's verse was dull, but the committee glimpsed a new and effective way of reading the Bible. Interest, the members thought, might be developed by encouraging people to restate scriptural ideas in verse. The best of these could be posted on the bulletin board and published in the parish newsletter.

While the committee was pursuing its inquiry, people were making out their federal income taxes before the April 15 deadline. To experiment with the method of putting the substance

of a passage in one's own words and idiom, a committee
member took Luke 16 and wrote this interesting if somewhat
disjointed verse:

> *My steward, let me see your book!*
> *Upon your balance let me look.*
> *Have you been faithful to my trust?*
> *Or has your soul been wrapped in rust?*
> *I see that Mammon got his share*
> *When God's allotment you did pare!*
>
> *You don't feel right*
> *When in my sight.*
> *Your alibi*
> *Comes to my eye.*
> *You've split your soul—*
> *Fum-ble-d your goal*
> *Served masters two*
> *Cut me from you.*
>
> *You cannot serve two masters, man.*
> *By your shrewd scheme you've built a plan*
> *That sells your soul as slave to taste*
> *Which all your talents tax and waste.*
>
> *My steward, check your book again.*
> *What standard ought to guide you men?*
> *Do you love Mammon more than me?*
> *My steward, can I count on thee?*

Another member of the committee, eyes now alert for the quest,
discovered that Elton Trueblood had put the Ten Command-
ments in verse to read like this:

> *Above all else love God alone;*
> *Bow down to neither wood nor stone.*
> *God's name refuse to take in vain;*
> *The Sabbath rest with care maintain.*
> *Respect your parents all your days;*
> *Hold sacred human life always.*
> *Be loyal to your chosen mate;*
> *Steal nothing, neither small nor great.*
> *Keep to the truth in word and deed;*
> *And rid your mind of selfish greed.*

In further study of Wesley's methods, the subcommittee dug up information about Wesley's custom of "abstracting," or "collecting"—as the activity was known in Oxford. This meant a habit of analysis of a passage and concise restatement in prose. It felt that here was an idea deserving of further thought. Then the subcommittee explored the group method which Wesley utilized at Oxford. A student group met at a regular time. It planned Scripture readings in advance, discussed them in the group, and developed personal application. The committee felt that time schedules, specific reading assignments, and the stimulation of group experience might be helpful.

Another subcommittee reviewed the devotional writings of William Law. They were especially impressed with his discussions of the close relationship between Bible reading and prayer. It took especial note of Law's use of a Psalm as introductory to prayer. By its subcommittee studies of Scripture-reading experience as a means of resource input, the committee began to see substantial approaches to its problems. It began to inventory and evaluate methods.

One member proposed that newspapers be studied to see points at which the Bible might have an application to events. Another suggested weekly mailing of assignments to each family, together with an overview of concepts to look for, applications to be made. Still another member proposed that the minister mail out his sermon topics for the entire eight-week period in advance.

It is sufficient to say that out of the committee's effort there developed a program for a Bible-emphasis reading period. This program as recommended to the Council was the result of thorough exploration made possible by the subdivision of the major problem and the assignment of the subsidiary problems for subcommittee study.

The product of the problem-group activity produced change: families of the church community began again to read the Bible with enjoyment; this activity strengthened the process of communication with God; it created a renewed awareness of religious values in everyday life. The church operating as a group workshop had strengthened the whole fabric of religious living.

THE PROBLEM: CONGREGATIONAL RENEWAL

Another case history will indicate the way a problem is stated and how it subdivides into subsidiary questions which require subcommittee study.

First United Church represents a merger of two once fashionable Presbyterian and Congregational churches in the formerly aristocratic Avondale and Walnut Hills suburbs in Cincinnati. As the older and wealthier families died out and the younger families moved to new suburbs, two churches sought survival by combining. Meanwhile the population of the community continued to undergo change. Protestantism became a minority faith, until ninety-six out of every hundred families were non-Protestants. The predominant background of the population came to be Jewish. In one census tract the Negro population increased seven and a half times in ten years. In another census tract area the influx of white population generally referred to as "hillbillies" began to supplant the Negro.

The religious services in the neighborhood were supplied by ten Jewish congregations, two huge Roman Catholic parishes, a Greek Orthodox church, six Protestant churches: an ultra-high Episcopal church, a Unitarian church, a New Jerusalem church, a Church of God, a storefront church, and the First United Church.

Population studies showed that the neighborhood was growing slowly and would stabilize about 1970. The residential section of the area was composed of one- and two-family houses with a median date of construction in the year 1910 and an average rental of $57.11 a month. The area contained the largest concentration of newer large multiple family housing units in the Queen City. The population was chiefly professional, technical, managerial, sales, and crafts. The number of widowed and divorced women outnumbered men four to one. Avondale was also a point of entry in the city for young men and women beginning their careers.

Geographically, Avondale had many advantages. It was the suburb most convenient to the downtown business area. It had good transportation and outstanding educational facilities. The University of Cincinnati was five minutes away. St. Xavier University was within walking distance. The area had a good park, a playground, excellent shopping facilities, a branch library, a golf course, a bowling alley, and a motion picture theater. It was served by excellent shopping facilities. Such were the realities of the situation.

PROBLEM SUBDIVISION

First United Church faced a crisis in its life. There were a number of alternatives. It had already tried merger when the Presbyterian and Congregational churches combined their ebbing strength. The congregation could sell its property and relocate. It could develop a neighborhood program appealing to the various segments of the population. It could turn its property over to a Negro group and disband. It could struggle along, with accelerating attrition, to certain death.

While the church was facing the choice among alternative and undesirable choices, the congregation called a new pastor. He proposed the exploration of one more alternative: *congregational renewal* to be achieved by mobilizing the resources of the church as a group workshop.

The Church Council proposed to find out whether the membership was really in earnest, not about First United alone, but about the mission and meaning of the Christian Church. It began its exploration of "the importance of taking the church in earnest" by proposing a new level of stewardship for the support of an enlarged ministry. A study of member families showed that 38 per cent contributed nothing to the church. There was a net loss of giving families of 8 per cent in the previous fiscal year. Of the 62 per cent of the families who did pledge to the church, 80 per cent were token givers, contributing two dollars a week or less to the church budget. The exploration of the alternative of congregational renewal therefore involved the answer to an important question: How much in *dollars* do our people believe in the mission of First United? The church took as a slogan "First United—Now Forward!" The families answered Yes. They pledged support to the alternative of congregational renewal.

The restructuring of the program of the church then began in earnest. The work involved fundamental decisions on policy. The people had decided by their pledges on congregational renewal *at the present site!* The church property itself

was in excellent condition. It possessed adequate facilities for
meeting the demands of almost any community need.

The renewal of the congregation proceeded with the development of problem-centered groups dealing with special
phases of the total project. One group began research on the
community resources. By the use of the studies of the Cincinnati Planning Commission, the census tract reports, Frederick
Shippey's *Church Work in the City*, and Edward Thorndike's
Your City, the task force completed a study of the community.
Other task forces worked long and hard. One studied area development and real estate values. It found in Chicago's North
Michigan Avenue concept of the "magnificent mile" an in-
triguing idea. Another committee dealt with recreational resources; another with working mothers. As the studies proceeded, it was recalled that a lot of experience showed that
in order to help people, "you yourself must have experienced
their problems." Alcoholics Anonymous was such an organization. Divorcees Anonymous was another. Recovery, organized
to help persons suffering from mental illnesses, was still another example. Forty Plus, a co-operative society of older men
mutually pledged to assist one another in finding jobs, likewise
was an example of the same principle at work.

First United proposed to put this principle to work. How
could the church serve the young unmarried adults who moved
into the community? Here was work for a problem-centered
group composed of young unmarried adults. How could the
church serve the widows and divorced women best? Two more
task forces were needed. What of the working mothers? They
wanted a pre-kindergarten Christian day school. The church
had already tried this activity and failed. Why had it failed
in the face of an urgent demand? Study showed that the previous school had been conducted as a sort of concession outside the organic life of the church. A clear functional division
was necessary between business and educational responsibility.
What of the service to the racial groups which composed the
community? One by one the problems were studied by appropriate task forces to discover the kind of program that
would provide a total effective ministry.

THE ECUMENICAL OUTLOOK

As the church continued its self-study it discovered that its lines of thinking fitted into the ecumenical pattern set by the topics for discussion at the Second Assembly of the World Council of Churches at Evanston. The six fields were:

1. Faith and Order—Our Oneness in Christ and Our Disunity as Churches
2. Evangelism—The Mission of the Church to Those outside Her Life
3. Social Questions—The Responsible Society in a World Perspective
4. International Affairs—Christians in the Struggle for World Community
5. Intergroup Relations—The Church Amid Racial and Ethnic Tensions
6. The Laity—The Christian in His Vocation

This gave the thinking in the congregation an organizational pattern.

"Here in Avondale," said First United Church to its neighborhood, "is a microcosm of divided Christendom. Let us come to know ourselves better." Youth groups began a program of study of the other religions in the area. They visited other churches, synagogues, temples, and storefronts. They studied likenesses and differences. They found areas of common heritage, usage, and co-operation.

Likewise First United found need for evangelism at its own dooryard. The invasion of the storefront church was one evidence of the opportunity. Racial and intercultural marriages tended to pull some families outside the religious societies. Some children of these families were already enrolling in church youth organizations at First United. "Our mission to those outside the life of the church?" observed one elder, "Avondale is a fertile field for evangelism!" Again, First United stood in the very midst of the predicament of racial and ethnic tensions. Here was an unparalleled opportunity for a ministry in reconciliation and fellowship. Finally, the renewal of First United congregation was predicated on a deepened awareness of the Christian in his vocation.

In the group workshop activity over a period of months, First United Church transformed itself from being a "problem church in a problem area" to a vital religious society aware of its mission and organized to deal with the opportunities that surrounded it on every side. Its difficulties had been turned into doors. It faced up to reality, drew upon available resources, developed new technologies, changed the culture of the group. By problem-centered work groups, First United demonstrated the resourcefulness of the human group to achieve positive change—to rejuvenate itself.

THE PROBLEM: COMMUNITY COLLEGE

The workshop church inevitably reaches out into the community to make prayed-for ideals concrete goals in the life of the city. The activity by which a church mobilizes its resources to make the ideal the real may be called *the executive function*. By defining ideals in terms of a sequence of concrete, achievable goals, the church elevates the life of a neighborhood to a new quality in living. To demonstrate the method by which a church in the spirit of love and reverence for people works for the achievement of the ideal, this third case history discusses a program of community action designed to explore the need for a community college.

The consideration of the possible need for a community college stems from a reading of population statistics. By 1970, it is estimated, the youth of college age will be double the number in 1943. Statistics indicate that half of the graduates from the upper half of the high school senior class do not go to college. Could the organization of a community college provide more educational opportunity for youth whose economic circumstances discourage higher education? Would a community college provide terminal programs of benefit to young men and women who do not desire a four-year course? How beneficial would a community college be in continuing adult education?

The question about the service of a community college was raised by a group in the Centreville Community Church. The subject was brought before the session of the church for a thorough discussion. While expressing no opinion, the session authorized a committee to proceed with the discussion, provided the intent to explore was fully explained to the superintendent of schools, the chairman of the school board, and the mayor. The minutes of the session read like this:

> The session authorizes a committee to explore the need for, problems related to, and anticipated benefits of a community college, provided the subject of exploration is fully explained to the superintendent of schools, the chairman of the school board, and the mayor. In taking this action, the session specifically points out that this subject interests the church because of its concern for equality of opportunity, the elimination of economic barriers to equal opportunity, the welfare of the community, and its general concern for the personal growth, spiritual development, and civic usefulness of people.

The position of the session was clear. The church had an obligation to act on the community level *when the case relates to human welfare and personal growth.*

Problem Subdivision

The committee proceeded to divide the general subject into smaller units which could be studied by functional task force committees. These committees took assignments of the following topics:

1. What happens to graduates of Centreville High School? This study included a ten-year analysis of graduates, the level of their ability, their continuation to college, their employment.
2. What will be the demand for higher education in Centreville in the next fifteen years?
3. Would a community college benefit Centreville industry?
4. What physical, financial, and educational resources would be required to establish a community college?
5. What has been the experience of other cities with a community college?

The study committee, staffed by representative community leaders with special acquaintance with the various topics, proceeded to explore. The members had no cut-and-dried answers. At this point they only wanted facts.

The facts as they fitted together did show the need for a community college. At each step in the development of the report, the various committees shared their growing body of information with people in the community—no matter whether they favored or opposed the idea. In the minds of the study groups there was only one question: Will the community college help Centreville to encourage the growth of people?

Granted the need, the committee next wanted to know whether Centreville was ready to take the step. To communicate the information which the committees had developed, the session now authorized a public meeting, the program for which is given in Figure 5. At this time the general committee wanted to make a public report and then release its study for general reading. It wanted to see how ready the community was to act on the need. From the time of this meeting, the community college movement in Centreville assumed a new pattern. While the church took a special interest in the progress of the movement, the committee knew that the subject now had become a public question! It knew that the movement now would require persistent educational support.

The public phase of the movement in Centreville became a record of the growth of civic opinion and technical detail. The church committee, still reporting regularly to the session, continued its quiet and sincere activity to keep the program moving forward on the public front. It broadened its scope to include membership from all segments of the community. The enlarged group, representing the whole community, took a new name: Centreville Citizens United for a Community College. The formation of the united front did not lessen the interest of the session in the achievement of the ideal.

From these representative and widely different case histories it can be seen how workshop problems are formulated and how the study of the major problem subdivides into task missions for further study and report. The exploration of these task missions gives depth to participation.

Figure 5. **PROGRAM PLANNING WORKSHEET**

Date: October 24 { Begin 8:00 P.M.
{ End 9:30 P.M.

SUBJECT: Will a community college benefit the people of Centreville?

PLACE: Centreville Community Church, Broadway and Second Street

OBJECTIVES OF MEETING

BEHAVIOR	CONTENT	METHOD
To give an overview of the	Community College	Dr. John Q. Doe, executive secretary, American Association of Junior Colleges
To summarize the need and requirements for a	Centreville Community College	Overview of committee report
To provide open discussion for	general expression of views	Interview panel headed by Judge T. E. Hughes

COMMON EXPERIENCES REQUIRED

A. PRESENTATION TO GROUP: Overview speech by Dr. John Q. Doe

B. PARTICIPATION BY GROUP:
1. Five minutes free time after film and speaker for collection of questions
2. Buzz groups after speaker to formulate interview questions for panel

RESOURCES NEEDED

A. PEOPLE—Roles

Personnel	Preparation
Ushers .... Waldo Haldeman, head usher	To select 12 ushers to report for conference and directions at 7:30 P.M.
Elkhart Community College Band ......:	To have 60 chairs ready
Projector ...... Harry Rood, director	To set up machine, screen, and check film before 7:15
Sexton ...... Russell I. Williams, Jr.	To have auditorium opened at 6:45 P.M.
Speaker ...... Willard Morris	To be met by Rodney Ellis; expected at airport Flight 36, arriving at 6:30, taken to dinner, attended, and taken to
John Q. Doe	airport to catch Flight 63 at 10:15 P.M.

Roles	Personnel (continued)	Preparation
Chairman	O. H. Clough, M.D.	
Buzz Group organizer	Fred Cousins	
Interview panel	Judge T. E. Hughes	
	Professor James Elson	
	Miss Anna Hunter	

B. FINANCES	Personnel	Preparation
Treasurer; 4 women at registration desk..	E. K. Jones, treasurer	Budget preparation and control; desk or table; cash box for fees; cards and schedules
	Ellen Leonard, registrar	
Committee of 3 on book sales table......	John Hull, book table	Table; green cover; supplies in by October 23

C. MATERIALS	Description	Preparation
Display posters	Four community colleges	Placed in hall bulletin board on October 17
Film	Elkhart Junior College at Work	To be shipped to Russell I. Williams, Jr.
Cards for questions		Head usher to obtain from pastor's secretary
Centreville report (printed by Knable's Mimeographing Service)		To be delivered to book table before 4:00 P.M.
The Community College (published by McGraw-Hill Book Company)		10 copies on consignment

PROMOTION

General Chairman, Mrs. Rutherford Haynes

Medium	Sub-Chairmen	Task
Church bulletin, newspaper, and bulletin boards	Miss Joyce Parker	To have announcements in church publication beginning two weeks before
Radio announcements	James Horn	To get announcements as often as possible
Newspaper stories and reports of meeting	Mrs. Ruth Porter	To get news in paper
Post card announcements	Mrs. John Bell	To be sent to each family in church
Posters	Miss Ethel Smith	To be made and put in windows by Girl Scouts
Telephone cascade	Merrill Beebe	To call 5 people, each of whom will call 5, each of whom will call 5 on agreed-upon name list
Personal Promotion—men	Dewey Potter	To have 10 men who will personally see 10 men each on agreed-upon list
Personal Promotion—women	Mrs. Rutherford Haynes	To have 10 women who will personally see 10 women each on agreed-upon list
Personal Promotion—high school	James Wallace	To have 10 high school students invite 10 high school students on agreed-upon list
Display in Insurance Company window	E. R. Painter	To provide a public exhibit and announcement

Readings

PROBLEM: BIBLE READING

Akin, Fessenden, Larson, and Williams, *Helping the Bible Speak*. New York: Association Press, 1956.

American Bible Society, *The Pastor and Ways of Using the Bible* (booklet). New York: American Bible Society.

Clinton, Kenneth, *Let's Read the Bible*. New York: The Macmillan Company, 1953.

Douglass, Paul F., *Wesleys at Oxford*. Bryn Mawr: Bryn Mawr Press, 1953.

Grant, Robert M., *The Bible in the Church*. New York: The Macmillan Company, 1948.

Huszar, George B., *Practical Applications of Democracy*. New York: Harper & Brothers, 1954.

Love, Julian Price, *How to Read the Bible*. New York: The Macmillan Company, 1945.

Oursler, Fulton, *The Greatest Story Ever Told*. New York: Permabooks, 1953.

Reeves, James, editor, *The Holy Bible in Brief*. New York: The New American Library of World Literature, 1954.

Ross, Murray G., *Religious Beliefs of Youth*. New York: Association Press, 1950.

Rowley, H. H., *The Relevance of the Bible*. New York: The Macmillan Company, 1944.

The following materials are available from the American Bible Society, Bible House, 450 Park Avenue, New York 22, N. Y.:

BOOKLETS: *The English Bible and the Life and Ideals of the English-speaking Peoples; The English Bible and British and American Art; A Ready Reference History of the English Bible.*

COLOR POSTERS: The Book to Live By; The Bible—A Light and Guide.

FILMSTRIPS AND MOTION PICTURES: *The Good Book*, 35 mm. color filmstrip, 22 minutes; *Our Bible—How It Came to Us*, 16 mm. sound, 84 minutes; *Bible on the Table*, 16 mm. sound, 28 minutes.

PROBLEM: CONGREGATIONAL RENEWAL

Bilheimer, Robert S., *The Quest for Christian Unity*. New York: Association Press, 1952.

Fisher, Galen M., *John R. Mott: Architect of Co-operation and Unity*. New York: Association Press, 1952.

Kendall, Guy, *The Social Applications of Christianity*. London: Gerald Duckworth & Company, 1948.

Knowles, Malcolm S., *Informal Adult Education*. New York: Association Press, 1950.

Latourette, Kenneth Scott, *The Emergence of a World Christian Community*. New Haven: Yale University Press, 1949.

Man's Disorder and God's Design. New York: Harper & Brothers, 1949.

Nichols, James H., *Evanston, an Interpretation*. New York: Harper & Brothers, 1955.

The Christian Hope and the Task of the Church. New York: Harper & Brothers, 1954.

Thorndike, Edward L., *Your City*. New York: Harcourt, Brace & Company, 1939.

Visser 't Hooft, W. A., *The First Assembly of the World Council of Churches*. New York: Harper & Brothers, 1954.

PROBLEM: COMMUNITY COLLEGE

Axt, Richard G., *The Federal Government and Financing Higher Education*. New York: Columbia University Press, 1952.

Bogue, Jesse P., *The Community College*. New York: McGraw-Hill Book Company, 1950.

Dahir, James, *Communities for Better Living*. New York: Harper & Brothers, 1950.

Fretwell, Elbert K., Jr., *Founding Public Junior Colleges*. New York: Teachers College, 1954.

Hollinshead, Byron S., *Who Should Go to College*. New York: Columbia University Press, 1952.

Millett, John D., *Financing Higher Education in the United States*. New York: Columbia University Press, 1952.

Sumption, Merle R., *How to Conduct a Citizens School Survey*. New York: Prentice-Hall, Inc., 1952.

5.

Involving People in Functional Roles:

THE TASK FORCES

The minister of the Bryn Mawr Presbyterian Church said
frankly to his congregation one Sunday morning:

> One of the great responsibilities of my pastorate lies in my
> awareness of our mutual need to involve our people in
> functional roles. Here we are—thousands strong. Our
> physical plant is magnificent—yet it stands idle much of
> the week. Many of our members, I know, are hungry to
> perform some mission to which they can devote their
> hearts and skills. Many others of us have heavy demands
> upon our time but are ready to serve on the line of duty
> —when and if there is a real need for our work. In our
> congregation we have a vast body of professional, scien-
> tific, academic, and business leadership. How can we
> challenge and channel our power under God's guidance
> to serve our needy world? [He paused.] It has been sug-
> gested to me that we organize here an Institute of Reli-
> gious Research. Think of the many points on which we
> could study and act. What should be the relationship of
> religion to the campus? How are religion and medicine
> mutually helpful? What is the relation of Christianity to
> industry? Can you see? Organized as task forces we could
> make a signal contribution to American thought and ac-
> tion by involving our people in functional roles.

He had stated a major problem; he had indicated how it could
be broken down into sub-problems, task forces, and participant
roles. He had, in fact, put his finger on a great need and responsibility: the obligation of the church to enrich its ministry by
the group workshop method.

The need which the distinguished Bryn Mawr pastor sensed

61

is general. The University of Michigan conducted a community study in metropolitan Detroit to discover the pattern of group involvement in that great industrial center. The survey brought out the fact that one out of every five persons belonged to no organization—that means 20 per cent of the population. Further, one out of seven had never belonged to an organization and did not live in a family having a single member belonging to a group. About one out of three persons belonged to a labor union. One person in eleven was involved in the activities of a church-connected group. Where group membership existed, the predominant pattern was that of the person who belonged to a labor union *and* a church group. Organized labor and organized religion thus provided the vehicle of experience through which people in Detroit most often joined together in formal groups.

Not only was participation in formal groups far less widespread than one might think; the Michigan study showed that the interest of members who did belong was none too vital. One out of four members of the organizations studied in Detroit did not attend a single meeting over a three-month period. Only two out of five members attended with any degree of regularity. One out of eight became complete deadheads. For this segment the group had provided inadequate role satisfaction.

The Michigan study further showed that participation and activity in groups tended to vary directly with age, education, and income. By age groups, active interest increased from the twenties through the forties, dropped in the fifties, and declined in the sixties. Thus, the vast need of the senior citizens was neglected. By education, membership and activity varied directly with the years of school completed. By income, membership and activity moved directly with ages and salaries earned. More than three times as many persons with incomes over $8,000 a year belonged to groups as those with incomes under $3,000. The former group attended and participated almost three times as much as the latter group. Finally, the Michigan study showed that the more active people become in groups, the more frequently they discuss politics, register to vote, and perform citizen duties.[1] Obviously, activity generates activity. People get in the habit of doing things by doing them. Participation encourages participation. The habit of participation gives zest and interest to living.

How People Become Involved in Functional Roles

A case history will show how people become involved in functional roles. Their acceptance of participant roles must come from heartfelt interest in response to genuine challenge. No artificial operations answer the need.

The story of the development of the library in the Broad Street Methodist Church, Kingsport, Tennessee, will indicate a natural pattern of evolution. When the congregation occupied its new church plant, the pastor mentioned that he had "a dream about a library." The National Council of Churches refers to a functional church library as "a positive help." The minister conceived of a working collection of books that would serve as reference and collateral reading to support the program of the various groups of the church. Further, he hoped that the circulation of books would serve as a means for communicating ideas about church-related subjects.

The pastor's dream moved toward realization during a session of a woman's group. A speaker emphasized the importance of "using your talents—now." A public school librarian felt herself "addressed." She volunteered her services to work on a committee to develop a report for the Commission on Christian Education. After careful study the committee made a report discussing ten ways in which a church library can serve a congregation. "A church library serves the people," said the report, "by providing (1) resource books for specialized activities, (2) reference books, (3) devotional classics, (4) current readings on religious subjects, (5) rental volumes in current demand, (6) selected magazines, (7) important pamphlets and reports, (8) indexed clippings on important subjects, (9) audio-visual aids, and (10) book review programs for the communication and discussion of ideas.

In the same report the committee gave its findings on the conditions which make for a good church library. "A good church library (1) is operated by a library committee responsible to an authoritative body of the church and by a qualified volunteer librarian with executive functions, (2) defines clear policies for its program designed to serve all the groups which comprise the congregation, (3) has attractive, if not always adequate, space, (4) has a budget and a program for developing 'Friends of the Library,' (5) makes book accessions selectively, giving the collection quality before quantity, (6) accepts no books which do not strengthen the collection, (7) catalogs books with an adequate classification system, (8) schedules hours to be open before and after major church meetings, (9) keeps people informed about its services, books, and materials, (10) displays material to encourage use of the library, (11) has a minimum of rules, (12) develops special library services as personnel becomes available, such as story hours for children, puppet shows to communicate ideas, recordings for circulation, and even art and handicraft exhibits, (13) recognizes that its function is to strengthen the resources of the church group, and (14) understands that its unique function is to encourage reading as a way to increase knowledge about God, his presence among men, and his work in the life of the world."

In its conclusions the committee made a catalog of the functional roles which would have to be filled to operate the service. "A church library," it said, "has need of roles to (1) staff the library committee, (2) staff the library service, (3) carry on public relations activity to encourage use of the library, (4) develop friends of the library to contribute funds and books, (5) circulate reading material to people confined to their homes, (6) maintain liaison with public and school librarians, (7) develop specialized areas of library service, (8) select visual aids and help in their use, (9) maintain the pamphlet service, (10) maintain the clipping file, (11) provide a reference service, (12) keep the budget control and financial records, (13) perform secretarial duties, (14) assist various groups with book review programs, and (15) provide liaison with church groups."

The report was adopted by the Commission on Education, which at the same time authorized the creation of a library committee. The Official Board appropriated $100 a year to support the new service. Presently a "Friends of the Library" group sprang up to acquire additional books and materials. A volunteer staff of ten was soon at work. Young people offered their services to staff the desk. The library committee, working with and reporting to the Commission on Education, defined the library policy and selected the books.

Since the central purpose of the library was a spiritual concern, the Kingsport church dedicated the new library by using a service developed by the National Council of Churches. That "Act of Dedication" was expressed in these words:

> In the name of God the Father Almighty, and in the presence of this congregation, we now dedicate this library to the glory of God.
>
> We dedicate this library to the service of little children, of whom such are the kingdom of God, that their minds, while young and formative, may learn to love, enjoy, and appreciate the things that are beautiful and good and true.
>
> We dedicate this library to parents that they may find help in building Christian homes filled with love and faith and trust in God and in each other.
>
> We dedicate this library to youth that their enthusiasm may be combined with wisdom and knowledge about God and worship, personal relations, leisure and recreation, avocations and vocations, man and society, and all fields of Christian living.
>
> We dedicate this library to the workers and members of the church school; to students who are seeking to learn of Christianity; to teachers who have given their lives to service and are seeking help and guidance to make their work more effective.
>
> We dedicate this library to all members of this church that they may find here wholesome reading for pleasure and profit and for the continual development of Christlike living.
>
> We dedicate this library to our community, that it may be a means of service and uplift to everyone and play a part in bringing here the kingdom of God.
>
> We dedicate this library to God, that it may be a means of continual service to the building of his kingdom.

THE ADMINISTRATION OF ROLE RESPONSIBILITY

When the role is recognized as the unit in the functional church, the *administration of role responsibility* becomes a primary obligation of the ministry. The First Baptist Church of Winston-Salem has developed a comprehensive program of role administration to include:

1. An up-to-date and continually revised schedule of roles listing as completely as possible all types of functional positions in the life of the church
2. A regularly scheduled systematic survey of the interests and capabilities of the constituency of the church
3. A card catalog record of the interest, capabilities, and experience of each person
4. A cumulative service record showing how responsibilities have been shared among qualified people
5. An organized system providing for the systematic enlistment of people into the groups within the church
6. An organized system of training providing for the communication of skills and understanding necessary to perform the respective roles

One of the methods of discovering people's interests is the use of the Talent Search Record shown in Figure 6. Many churches make use of schedule sheets like the one used by the Winston-Salem Church. Some churches include special roles. The Bryn Mawr (Pennsylvania) Presbyterian Church, for example, includes such a role as blood donor and keeps a record of blood types for the aid of members of the congregation who may need blood transfusions. It also includes special interest groups, such as photography and a roster of professional men and women in the medical, dental, psychiatric, nursing, and legal professions who stand ready to be of service to needy persons. It is necessary to remember, however, that the church is a dynamic group. Hence its roles cannot be stereotyped, although many of them are permanent requirements in the life of the church.

Within the life of the First Baptist Church there are six hundred roles which are classified as elective. The church spells out its policies concerning the nomination of individuals to hold office. These policies are:

1. No member, except the treasurer, shall hold more than one church-elected office concurrently.

2. No member shall serve as Sunday School superintendent, Training Union director, or as chairman of a committee more than three consecutive years.
3. All officers are elected to serve for a period of one year beginning on October 1 and ending on September 30.
4. Trustees, senior deacons, and junior deacons are elected for three-year terms.

Figure 6. **TALENT SEARCH RECORD**

FIRST BAPTIST CHURCH, WINSTON-SALEM, NORTH CAROLINA

NAME. . . . . DATE. . . . .

RESIDENT ADDRESS . . . . .TEL. . . . .

BUSINESS ADDRESS . . . . TEL. . . . .

OCCUPATION—PROFESSION . . . .

Please check below if you have engaged in or are willing to engage in the following opportunities of Christian service:

Have Done	Will Do	Have Done	Will Do
SUNDAY SCHOOL		**CHURCH OFFICERS AND COMMITTEES**	
____General Superintendent	____	____Church Clerk	
____General Associate	____	____Church Treasurer	____
____Department Superintendent	____	____Church Librarian	____
____Department Associate	____	____Usher	
____Teacher—What age?____	____	____Greeter	
____Gen. or Dept. Secretary	____	____Trustee	____
____Cradle Roll Visitor	____	____Deacon	____
____Extension Visitor	____	____Junior Deacon	____
____Vacation Bible School	____	____Baptism Committee	____
____Class Officer	____	____Building Committee	____
____Mission Sunday School	____	____Contact Committee	____
____Nursery Worker	____	____Evangelism Committee	____
		____Finance Committee	____
TRAINING UNION		____Flower Committee	____
		____Hospitality Committee	____
____General Director	____	____House and Grounds Committee	____
____General Associate	____	____Library Committee	____
____Department Director	____	____Lord's Supper Committee	____
____Department Associate	____	____Church Ministries Committee	____
____Counselor	____	____Missions Committee	____
____Leader	____	____Music Committee	____
____Sponsor	____	____New Member Committee	____
____Union Officer	____	____Nominating Committee	____
____Mission Training Union	____	____Nursery Committee	____
____Nursery Worker	____	____Publicity Committee	____
		____Scouting Committee	____
		____Youth Committee	____

Have Done   Will Do   Have Done   Will Do

W. M. U.

____President   ____
____Young People's Director   ____
____First Vice-President   ____
____Second Vice-President   ____
____Recording Secretary   ____
____Corresponding Secretary   ____
____Treasurer   ____
____Committee Chairman   ____
____B.W.C. Adviser   ____
____Circle Chairman   ____
____Y.W.C. Counselor   ____
____G.A. Counselor   ____
____R.A. Counselor   ____
____Sunbeam Band Leader   ____
____Sunbeam Baby Visitor   ____
____Mission W.M.U.   ____

PERSONAL

My Hobby or Hobbies: _____

_____

What I Would Like to Do Most in My

Church: _____

_____

_____

My Second Choice: _____

_____

MUSIC

____Solo Work   ____
____Choral Work   ____
____Directing   ____
____Play Piano   ____
____Play Organ   ____
____Play _____   ____

SPECIAL SERVICES

____Typing   ____
____Telephoning   ____
____Transportation   ____
____Operate Motion Picture Pro-
jector   ____
____Woodwork and Handcraft   ____
____Coach Sports   ____
____Direct Games   ____
____Plan Socials   ____
____Give Readings   ____
____Storytelling   ____
____Soul Winning   ____
____Make Posters   ____
____Aid in the Kitchen   ____
____Operate Mimeograph   ____
____Interior Decorating   ____
____Painting
____Direct Plays and Pageants   ____
____Act in Plays and Pageants   ____
____Make-Up Artist   ____
____Set Designer (Stage)
____Electrical Knowledge   ____
____Operate Public Address Sys-
tem   ____
____Playing Service Tape Record-
ings to Shut-ins   ____

On the basis of the hundreds of clearly defined roles which must be filled, a nominating committee, by the use of role files and the cumulative service records, makes proposals for election in a series of four conferences that spread the work over the entire summer in a systematic personnel program. These four personnel sessions are known as the June Conference; the July Conference; the August Conference; and the September Conference. The time which the First Baptist Church finds it necessary to devote to its "personnel" planning indicates the size of the task that must be performed when the church is operated as a "group workshop."

Involving people in functional roles in task-centered activity becomes a major administrative problem of the church. Quite as much as refinement of the policy and program, it requires, at the heart of the church organization, a *records system*.

Readings

Pleuthner, Willard A., *More Power for Your Church*. New York: Farrar, Strauss & Young, 1952.

Shippey, Frederick A., *Church Work in the City*. New York: Abingdon Press, 1952.

Your Church Library (booklet). Chicago: National Council of the Churches of Christ in the United States of America. Twenty-five cents.

6.

Administering the Church
as a Group Workshop:

THE GOAL-SETTING CONFERENCE

Discussion so far has dealt with the theory and mechanics of the workshop church. The theory is that the meeting ground of personality and society lies at that point of common effort where people in a face-to-face group squarely face a problem, think through a program which will provide a solution, and then execute the program by means of goal-directed and task-centered activity. The workshop is that point at which people combine their energies, share their intelligence, and pool their hearts' desires in a specific and common cause. This kind of activity where problems are brought to focus, questions asked, answers thought through, and action organized into task missions is the way human society operates; for society itself exists in communication.

In practice the operation of the church as a group workshop requires a keen appreciation of the nature of the person in the context of his group relationships, a mastery of the techniques of organization and administration, and awareness of how the workshop provides a vehicle of spiritual growth.

The administration of the workshop requires careful planning. During the writer's last visit with John R. Mott, this great master of the "workshop way" said this:

> Write this down, Douglass, and underline it twice. *Successful meetings do not come by accident. Great spiritual change does not result from magic.* Neither is ever accidental. Both result from prayer, planning, and attention to detail. ATTENTION TO DETAIL! Few meetings can rise above the quality of the vision, the adequacy of the preparation, and the sincerity of the intercession. I have

70

always made it a matter of urgent policy to make careful and painstaking preparation in advance of every meeting. Personally I have always inspected all the physical arrangements for furthering the comfort, the understanding, and the response of people—including seating, ventilation, light, note paper, pencils, and provision for recording the productivity of the group through minutes and findings. I have always worked out group understandings and agreements on rules of operation. Failure to attend to just one simple detail may ruin the possibilities of a whole meeting.

The whole purpose of convening a meeting is to move forward—now. A meeting is only a stepping stone. It turns stumbling blocks (problems) into stepping stones (solutions). Its purpose is to explore ideas, agree on a course of action, and translate a vision into an achievement. A meeting which is not moving a cause forward is letting the world career backwards. I have never proposed to be a party to any such kind of performance. Of course you've seen the inscription on the campus sundial:

> *The shadow by my finger cast*
> *Divides the future from the past;*
> *Before it stands the unborn now*
> *In darkness, and beyond thy power.*
> *Behind its unreturning line,*
> *The vanished hour, no longer there.*
> *One hour alone is in thy hands—*
> *The NOW on which the shadow stands.*

The purpose of life is to do something for God and man now—in our generation. Never let a lack of attention to detail be the cause of the failure of a meeting.

THE PAPER WORK

As has been suggested before, the management operation of the workshop requires detailed paper work. This merely means that the pattern of activity is clearly spelled out. Here are the steps necessary to make the organizational pattern firm and understandable.

1. Write out the *formulation of the problem* precisely.
2. Write out fully the *policy* of the group for dealing with

this problem so that it can be implemented by a program.

3. Define this program operationally in a series of working documents which include:

a. An *analysis of the roles* which need to be performed to achieve the goal stated in the policy statement. How many and what kinds of people are needed to fill the jobs? This analysis will provide an estimate of the personnel needed.

b. A description of the organizational pattern by means of an *organizational chart* which shows the relationship of roles to the whole.

c. An explanation of the duties of each position on the chart, by means of a *job or role description*.

d. The design of a *flow chart* to show the sequences of operations necessary to accomplish the purpose of the group.

e. A schedule of each operation for a specific date on an *operating calendar*.

f. A provision of *a plan for adequately communicating* the action program, the organizational pattern, the precise roles, persons assigned to those roles, and the purpose of the operation to the people concerned.

g. A schedule of adequate *training sessions*.

h. A *budget* worked out, adopted, and lived within.

i. A *plan for organizational reporting* so that the leaders can keep the operations under control in terms of goals.

j. A *system of achievement auditing* so that the production of the work group can be measured at all times in terms of achievement of policy goals.

k. An organization of all these working papers in an *operations manual* designed specifically for the whole group.

While the operating detail of each project requires careful definition, the church administrator, looking at his whole constituency, needs to have *a central and functional role cumulative service record* for all his people. This, as the experience of the First Baptist Church in Winston-Salem demonstrates, is the control point at which the church administrator can evaluate the needs of all his people and the success of the church in meeting those needs. This central file is the point at which the pastor thinks about all his people—not just those with whom he seems most frequently to come in contact.

THE GOAL-SETTING CONFERENCE

While the workshop way can be used in dealing with any problem at any meeting, it is possible for a church to undertake a thorough approach to the method through the instrumentality of a goal-setting conference.

The National Council of Churches suggests that a congregation may wisely make a self-audit by directing to itself some such questions as these:

1. "What should our church be accomplishing anyway?"
2. "What goals are we seeking?"
3. "Does our church have any goals?"[1]

After proposing these inquiries, the National Council goes on to say that "any person traveling in the country without a goal may wander here and there without getting anywhere." Goals give direction; yet, as the National Council points out, "thousands of local churches are doing little to reach the unreached about them, or to Christianize the communities of which they are a part, or even to serve adequately the people who regularly share in their service."

How does a church review its work and develop policies and programs by a thorough involvement of its people? Once a church has defined its goals, the church asks, "What program will achieve these goals?" Finally, as the National Council asks, "How will this kind of program help people to become the kind of person envisioned in the goals?" How does the church begin to plan a ministry through workshop groups?

On previous pages it has been pointed out that workshop groups ought to be organized into the organic structure of the church. They should never be activities which dangle aside from the central program of the church.

The adequate development of the group workshop pattern can perhaps best be carried on by means of a *goal-setting conference*. Such a conference is an organized over-all work group composed of church leaders—representatives from each organized group in the church. The conference becomes a project which involves all the people of the church in the *thinking-planning-doing activity* required to build a calendarized road map for the whole church year. The preparation for this kind of conference requires detailed staff work extending over many months. Once the authoritative church policy body has authorized the conference, the leaders need to think about a time schedule. The exploratory work may well begin in the fall for a conference which normally meets regularly in the spring for ten or twelve two-hour sessions.

In one form or another the working secretariat of the conference is divided into two task forces: the organizing committee; and the records and findings committee. These two committees, functioning often as a committee of the whole, perform the central development and steering operations. Adequately to prepare for the spring meetings, the organizing committee needs to undertake its preparatory work by late October. The membership of this task force may well include the largest contributor to the church, a person who has had policy-planning experience in industry, a person who has specialized in personnel, an accountant who is an expert at figures and details, and a secretary who takes shorthand and likes to write reports. In other words, the organizing group should have a functional rather than accidental competency. It should be one that involves new minds capable of taking a new but balanced look. Probably a committee of seven, with the pastor and lay leader of the church serving as ex officio members, will be most effective. By diplomatic and positive communication and stimulation, this group invites each organized group and functional service within the church to develop a good statement for presentation to the conference in the spring.

The organizing group asks the societies in the church to build their reports on a uniform pattern:

1. What has our group been doing? The question causes

the society to make a factual statement about its productive work.

2. Why did we do what we did? This question causes the society to go into the history of its activities and to evaluate its goals.

3. How have our activities contributed to the growth of people in (a) increased knowledge, (b) improved skills, (c) awareness of Christian values, and (d) Christian service?

4. What goals do we propose to set for ourselves next year?

5. What kind of a program will be required to achieve these goals?

In the study of these questions all the members of each group become involved in evaluating their performance and projecting their plan. The questions precipitate group self-study during the winter months. Co-operating closely with the various groups, the organizing committee consolidates the individual reports into a church-wide report built around the questions:

1. What has our church as a whole been doing?

2. Why did our church do what it did?

3. How have our total church activities contributed to the growth of people in (a) increased knowledge, (b) improved skills, (c) awareness of Christian values, and (d) Christian service?

4. What goals should our church set for itself to achieve in the next year?

5. What program in workshop groups will help to achieve these goals?

The National Council of Churches suggests a check sheet which may be helpful to the organizing committee in the preparatory analysis. This sheet is shown in Figure 7; it should, however, be used only as one tool, never as a definitive audit.

The goal-setting conference, scheduled for the spring, spreads its sessions over ten or twelve weeks. At the first session each group makes a brief report built around two questions:

Figure 7. CHURCH PROGRAM CHECK SHEET

Not every group listed will be found in every community; not every need will be met as well each year—the church serving through community agencies at times. — GROUPS FOR THE CHURCH TO SERVICE	1. Infants 1-3 yrs. Cradle-roll Nursery	2. Pre-school 4-5 yrs.	3. Primary Grades 1-3	4. Juniors Grades 4-6	5. Junior High Grades 7-9	6. High School Grades 10-12	7. College and Professional (Those away from home)	8. Employed Youth 18-24 yrs.	9. Young Adults 25-30 yrs. (unmarried)	10. Young married (without children) (with children)	11. Adult men	12. Adult women	13. Elderly Adults	14. Temporary residents	15. Racial minority 16. Non-resident members
NEEDS TO BE MET ADEQUATELY															
A. Opportunities for *Worship*															
a. as auditors in groups															
b. as participants															
c. as leaders, sharing in plans															
d. family and private devotions															
B. Opportunities for *Learning*															
a. Bible study and Christian living															
b. church history and doctrine															
c. missions and stewardship															
d. leadership training															
e. preparation for membership, for worship and service															
f. sex, pre-marital counseling															
C. Opportunities for *Fellowship*															
a. socials within groups															
b. socials between groups, church and community wide															
c. recreation, athletics, health															
d. hobbies, music, drama, etc.															
D. Opportunities for *Service* in the community–Scouts, PTA, citizenship, etc.															
E. *Wider* opportunities for *Service*															
a. denominational and district work															
b. inter-denominational contacts															
c. inter-religion contacts															
d. inter-national goodwill projects															
F. Specialized needs (if state fails), Day-school, vocational guidance, library housing, pastoral counseling, etc.															

Reprinted by permission, National Council of the Churches of Christ in the United States of America, from **Improving the Total Program of Your Church,** p. 7.

1. What have we been doing?
2. What do we propose to do?

At the end of this preliminary reporting, the conference members have been briefed on the activities of the whole church. Once these reports have placed the conference members on common ground, productive discussion commences. The tentative agendas for subsequent meetings begin to take shape. People start to explore ideas. The "group multiplier" goes to work. Ideas generated by the interpersonal interactions of the conference are fed back to the groups represented for reaction, criticism, and development.

The Integrating Plan

Out of the conference discussion emerges a provisional integrating plan and an organizational action calendar for the year. This plan is a compilation of the plans of all the groups which comprise the church. The omnibus plan needs to be submitted to the groups of the church for review, comment, and report. When the final draft of the report is completed, it is mimeographed. A copy is sent to each family of the church constituency. This wide distribution encourages discussion of the ideas in family circles.

PASTORAL EXPOSITION

To further explain the report, the pastor should devote a morning sermon hour to the subject. Such an exposition will provide him the opportunity to present an overview of the church at work.

THE CHURCH MEETING

A report which concerns all the people of the church should be discussed in a general meeting. In churches that provide for congregational authority, the report may be finally acted upon at this time. In churches that have an authoritative body other than the congregation, the action of the church meeting may be in the nature of an advisory recommendation.

For the church "as a whole" and "for each group in particular," the final program should be spelled out in a carefully prepared church manual that again provides for:

1. A statement of policy in achievable, operational terms
2. A plan for executing the policy presented as a detailed program which describes what specific steps are necessary to achieve the goals stated in the policy
3. A catalog of roles to be occupied by persons, together with a plan for enlisting and training the personnel required
4. A description of the materials required by the people performing the work of the group
5. An organizational diagram
6. A description of each job
7. A scheduling calendar
8. A budget
9. A plan for meetings
10. Provision for operational control
11. A program audit built from the policy goals and objectives to determine to what extent the goals have been achieved
12. A quarterly progress performance report

A church conducted as a group workshop requires the same quality of careful administration as that exercised in the program of a well-managed industry. When goals are sharply focused, roles clearly defined, programs developed in detail, and work performed by persons in groups with competent skills, high purposes are achieved.

Leadership Workshop and Practicum

To develop leadership equipped to strengthen the purposes of the church operating as a group workshop, it is necessary to make provision for training in participant group skills. The objectives of a leadership workshop and practicum, as Thelen says, are

> to train members to recognize . . . group processes . . . appropriate to the group task, what the consequences of different sources of processes are, how members contribute to determine the nature of the processes, how leaders effect these processes, how a group whose processes are inappropriate may be helped to improve. The task of the

trainer in such groups is to see to it that the group has significant experiences in trying to work together, and that conditions are such that people can learn from these experiences. . . . The aim of training is (a) to help people learn how to behave in groups in such a way that groups solve the problems for which they were assembled and (b) to insure that individuals have a meaningful, rewarding, and need-meeting experience. When both of these conditions are present simultaneously the individual is challenged and rewarded for creativity and insights, and the decisions reached by the group are wiser than those any one person could reach by himself. Thus, we might say briefly that the aim of training is simultaneously to help other groups become more effective instruments for social action, on the one hand, and, on the other, to help individuals to grow and learn.[2]

The training sessions should be developed on the workshop pattern, but these workshops must provide opportunity for the leadership trainees to practice the skills as they are studied.

The workshop and practicum is generally scheduled around the Labor Day holiday. This time has the advantage of leaving the group with fresh knowledge, skill, and enthusiasm at the threshold of the fall program of the church.

This leadership group becomes a team of specialists who go out as change-agents to catalyze human reactions in the various groups in the church, for each group has been asked to assign some of its members for leadership training.

Before the leadership trainees can become a team fighting to achieve a common goal (healthy, productive, God-centered groups), the associated individuals must be welded into an operating unity by a singleness of purpose. The cement of morale must bind the members of the leadership training group together. A oneness of purpose must dominate the mind and will of the separate individuals. The leadership team must be carried forward by a common inner compulsion. To communicate that single leadership idea is the task of the workshop-practicum. That idea must be shared so vividly that each member is fitted into the whole church objective by his own accord and with skill and enthusiasm. This task of bringing discrete human units into a striking force expressing a single leadership idea is a technical and difficult training function.

Jesus was pretty clear about the conditions necessary for doing this job of orientation, of communicating a compelling idea from one mind to the soul of a working group. He was sure that the job could not be done while men were working at their everyday tasks on their everyday docks, in their everyday boats, with their everyday business associates. He knew that at some point the quest for illumination demands that men break away from their routine, withdraw to a quiet conference place where they can be alone with one another and with ideas. Jesus demonstrated all this by taking his team away to the mountain. He arranged to take the disciples away to discuss the qualities of character of the kind of man he was talking about. He wanted a quiet time to talk things over, to discuss goals and roles. He wanted time for a "how-to-do-it session." He wanted to analyze the means by which a man grows in the image of God, to discuss change. So Jesus and his disciples stepped out of the routine day.

On the mountain Jesus opened the session by asking questions. Why does a man fail to achieve dignity in his inner being? Jesus stated his diagnosis in almost behavioristic terms. A man does not achieve character, he suggested, because he lives as a split personality. He wants two incompatible things at the same time and with equal intensity. He lacks internal coherence. And why? Because he lives as a divided self in a world which can be dealt with only by a singleness of soul. A man, he proposed, cannot act with integrity when he looks for external sanctions to support inner compulsions. A man cannot perform with intrinsic merit when he ignores the quality of his act and looks for approval in the eyes of his supervisor. A man is a hypocrite when he wants men to take note of how he acts as an index of the sincerity of his inmost soul.

What Jesus was saying to his men whom he had extricated from humdrum routine of the day by taking them to the mountain for orientation was that a man does not grow in character until he rises above himself, until he commits himself to a higher loyalty, until he associates himself with a higher source of goodness, until a larger universe moves in to reinforce his own and backs up his life purpose. There a man finds God.

Leadership goals can be achieved by the selection and assignment of people to fill roles on the team. The achievement of goals requires the multiplication of effort through the association of people in a common effort. It requires the recruitment of a team, the co-ordination of the activities of the team members by the organization of roles dominated by a common idea, and by the division of labor through the assignment of tasks necessary to carry out the common purposes. Jesus proceeded to recruit men to occupy leadership roles on his team.

While he was walking along the shores of the Sea of Galilee, he saw two brothers casting nets into the sea. Using their own idiom of speech he said to them in substance: "We've got a job to do together. It has to do with human beings rather than fish." And so a group organization began to take shape as four fishermen joined with one carpenter as leaders in a common enterprise. When Simon Peter, Andrew, James, and John left their nets and went with Jesus, they demonstrated the second fundamental principle of group action: involvement and participation in a working partnership.

Jesus recognized that no leader can be a man of action all the time if he is going to be an effective captain, executive, or administrator. Any man who leads and bears responsibilities for results must get away by himself to think, to plan, to meditate, to let ideas germinate into patterns and programs of action. A man must take time for renewal. Jesus practiced this rhythmical cycle of action and meditation. He was praying alone when his disciples—his staff—wanted to share in his quiet time. They wanted to find out the technique for talking with God. They wanted the how-to-do-it of inner experience. There come moments when every leader must share his inspiration, when he must rekindle the aspiration of his staff by reaffirming the common purpose of the group in a workable statement. There is need for a common creed, for a policy statement, for a new formulation of goals.

This is exactly what happened when the disciples said to the Master: "Lord, teach us to pray." Jesus answered by leading his staff in a common prayer, a new and common ritual which was to survive as one of the world-wide bonds of the Christian fellowship. This is the way to pray, said Jesus:

Our Father who art in heaven,
Hallowed be thy name. Thy kingdom come,
Thy will be done, on earth as it is in heaven.
Give us this day our daily bread. And forgive us
our trespasses, as we forgive those who trespass
against us. And lead us not into temptation, but
deliver us from evil.

The leadership workshop is just such a spiritual moment. Its purpose is to deal with the deepest motivations and highest aspirations of men as they express themselves in down-to-earth activities.

Within every leadership operation involving human performance there come times when that performance must be evaluated according to some standard. The staff, the leadership team around Jesus, wanted to have a standard yardstick to measure the value of leadership performance. Jesus gave them what they asked for. Here was his rule: "Whosoever of you will be the chiefest shall be servant of all: let him be your servant, even as the Son of man: for even the Son of man came not to be ministered unto but to minister, and to give his life a ransom for many."

In much of the current psychology there has been an effort to insist that people work with and through one another, but not *for* one another. In that preposition there seems to reside, so some psychologists now hold, a sense of "maternal" solicitude that makes one person intrude into the life of another in a way which prevents the latter from standing on his own feet. This was not the intention of Jesus. His point was that in working together, one person has to take a personal interest in another to create conditions in which the other person can be both normal and free. Jesus expected a leadership act to be performed, not from selfish reasons, but in the spirit of helpfulness and love, defined as the emotional urge which leads a person through positive action into immediate, personal, and helpful contact with others. What Jesus was setting up was the standard of unselfish leadership service. The quality of the love becomes the yardstick. It is expressed not only in the capacity to work with other people, but to work for other persons as well. It is the *"for"* that opens up the conditions which enable a person to exercise freedom and responsibility in his own life space. Personality in this sense becomes the capacity to work with and for other people. This, then, is a rule of action which helps men to remain humble. It is by this standard that the genuineness and integrity of everyone working in a group can be measured—by the extent to which one person opens up opportunities for another person to experience inner growth. This is the basic leadership function; its development is the purpose of the workshop and practicum.

If wholeness in participation is a goal, how can one judge the contribution a person makes when it is clearly recognized that every human being differs from every other in his abilities? How is one to judge the quantity of quality performance? Jesus recognized this problem too. By way of answer he cited the widow and her mite. Here was a human being who performed to the level of her ability. Jesus' answer was that what makes an act acceptable and divine is total performance with every resource a person can bring to the task. It is this maximum contribution in terms of every individual's maximum that counts. It is the completeness of participation that matters. The widow gave all that she had.

In his group work Jesus, too, was concerned with role playing. He wanted his leadership team to exchange places and look at themselves through the eyes of others. Such a frankness was the substance of the golden rule. Getting along with other people, Jesus said, is difficult until one man changes places with another man and looks at himself from the other's position. Such a procedure works an amazing therapy in human understanding. In the reversal of roles a man gets a broader understanding of himself than he would if he just went on living in the world circumscribed by his own understanding of himself.

However effective the fall leadership workshop and practicum may have been, short continuing refresher sessions and clinical sessions must be held throughout the year. Jesus recognized that in every group, every organization, and every church group workshop the players and staff members face situations and problems which discourage them. Things do not seem to be turning out right. At such times the leaders need to take steps to reassure their men. They need to talk things over, to study their mistakes, to plan a new attack, to inspire the added ounce of effort necessary to achieve a desired result. As in a game, the players need to break away from the routine of the contest for a critical look at performance. They need to go into a huddle to plan the next play.

Simon is an example of one who needed encouragement. He had toiled all night and caught no fish. Such failure was serious for him, because he earned his living by filling his net. Frustrated in daily tasks, he had already given up when Jesus urged him to try once more. At Jesus' encouragement he did try again—just once more. "Nevertheless," said Simon, "at thy word I will let down the net." That last time was enough. It produced results. Likewise in the workshop church the leadership corps faces difficult situations as they further the maturing of participation skills. Frequent huddles of the leadership group are necessary to maintain the effectiveness of the leadership corps. The Labor Day workshop-practicum is only one initial session. Subsequent sessions need to be staggered throughout the church year. The purposes of the leadership core group are always the same: to mature the trainee's competence as a participant in groups; and to improve his competence in communicating the ideals of participant skills to the workshop group to which he belongs.

Within any church the workshop groups will differ widely in their participant maturity. Hemphill has classified fifteen different dimensions of groups. Among these dimensions are *size, viscidity* (degree of "togetherness") and *cohesion, homogeneity* (age, common interest, economic status, cultural background, sex), *flexibility* (degree to which the group adheres to an established, persisting mode of behavior), *permeability* (degree to which the group sets itself off from those who do not belong, restrictions on membership), *polarization* (degree to which the group is oriented toward a clear definite goal), *stability* (degree to which major changes occur within group), *intimacy* (degree to which members are acquainted), *autonomy* (degree to which group is independent of other groups), *control* (degree to which the behavior of their members is regulated by membership in the group), *position* (status within group), *potency* (strength of the individual needs satisfied by group membership, role satisfaction), *hedonic tone* (general feeling of satisfaction, tone of pleasantness and agreeableness associated with membership), *participation* (depth of involvement in the group's work), and *dependence* (relationship between an individual member of a group and its leader).[3]

No two groups within the same church will present the same workshop situations. Thelen wisely points out that

> it is possible, for example, for a group whose members are mostly educated, well adjusted, and knowledgeable to get nowhere: consider many school faculty meetings. It is possible for administrators marvellously trained to be unable somehow to run successful staff meetings. It is possible for members of a community council, highly successful as leaders in their own organizations, to be unable to work together. It is possible for people trained in research and loaded with information about what happens in groups to be unable to contribute effectively to groups of which they are a part. It is even possible for a group, highly successful in planning policy for its organization's executive secretary, to fail miserably when its cooperation with other groups is required.[4]

Thelen goes on to say that the successful group in its operation must take into account "not only the characteristics of individuals but also the nature of the problem, the limitations of time and freedom of action imposed by the institution or community, and such group factors as morale, expectations, power fantasies, status in the community, and of the kind of group the members think it is. All these factors come together to determine the quality of experience the group will have, or to put it in other words, the nature of the 'group processes.' "[5]

The leadership workshop-practicum must be continuingly concerned with the relationship of the capabilities of the leadership corps, the dimensions of the group, and the demands of the situation.

TEACHING MOMENTS IN GROUP EXPERIENCE

In the problem-centered activities of the group, great moments of teaching opportunity present themselves. Hence the leader must not only be skilled in his capabilities in dealing with the group processes; he must also have a richness of personal command over biblical concepts and religious history. What are some of the concepts that can be and ought to be emphasized in giving the workshop group a sound religious orientation? Here are fifteen fundamental ideas which ought to be kept in mind by every person in the workshop group:

ORIGIN—man created by God in his own image.

RELATIONSHIP—God the father; man the son; neighbor the brother.

DESTINY—quest to find, to know, and to communicate with God.

PURPOSE—love of God and service of man.

STEWARDSHIP—use of life and possession as a God-given trust.

COMMITMENT—singleness and selflessness of purpose.

REVERENCE—worth of every man in God's love.

LOVE—self-giving in outreaching helpfulness.

MERCY—free and undeserved forgiveness abundant to man's needs.

CONTRITION—confession by man himself that at his best he falls far short of God's expectation and is unworthy of the fullness of God's grace.

MORALITY—man's "yes" response when the "ought-to-be" stands ever against the "is" and will not let it rest.

TRANSCENDENCE—God as more than his creation and other than man's self or the material universe; God is "the Beyond that is within."

IMMANENCE—the transcendent God as the available God at work in the world and in the inward experience of man. "I dwell in the high and holy place, with him also that is of a contrite and humble spirit."

ENCOUNTER—the event which occurs when God confronts man face to face with a moral situation to which he can make a "yes" response in the spirit of divine love and mercy.

CROSS—the event when one gives himself without reservation to meet another's need, as Jesus spent himself to reconcile man in fellowship with God.

A productive group deepens the roots of religious insight when its activities create an awareness of these concepts. Indeed,

Jesus used teaching moments in the group process for some of his greatest instruction. His method was principally the parable: a narration of well-known scenes or events close to the daily experience of the group members. From these familiar situational patterns he developed spiritual principles of action. His teaching in this way was vivid and rememberable. From the parable of the Pharisee and the publican, Jesus could show that a tax gatherer may be reverent, humble, and aware of his own spiritual plight. In the parables of the lost sheep and the lost coin he could show God's concern for the worth of every individual. To the Pharisee who criticized Jesus for eating with taxgatherers and sinners, Jesus could say that

> those who are strong have no need of a doctor, but those who are ill. Go and learn the meaning of this word, *I care for mercy, not for sacrifice.* For I have not come to call just men but sinners.[6]

Jesus was criticized for picking corn on the sabbath. He replied:

> If you had known what this meant, *I care for mercy, not for sacrifice,* you would not have condemned men who are not guilty.[7]

Jesus, it must be remembered, was concerned with communicating motivating ideas to ordinary people. He had no selected audiences; he established no Ivy League admission standards to his meetings. People came because they had curiosity to see and hear him. His instruction was directed to three kinds of persons: to his special pupils—his disciples—the inner staff circle which worked most closely with him; to the general public; and to individual persons. He engaged in no solo performances built around grand oratory. Jesus merely became one of the group. He sat down, and people gathered around him. There was silence and then he taught. He illustrated his principles by use of homespun stories built around the things with which ordinary people were familiar. He spoke with a knowledge of the past, but with a fresh insight into people's problems and a concern for their future.

Finally, it must be remembered that communication in a group breaks down most often at the point of personal "feelings." Feelings are indeed a very real fact. In human relationships these feelings take no secondary place in the educational process. Their existence for good or bad colors and gives tone to every other reaction. People who work with people must recognize the prime importance of feeling as it relates to personal roles and the achievement of group goals. As Brown says: "The perception of goals, as either desirable and hence to be sought after or as undesirable and hence to be avoided, always is experienced with emotion."[8]

Teaching is central in the administration of the church operated as a group workshop. The process begins at the moment that the workshop way is accepted; it never ends.

Readings

Ahern, Eileen, *Handbook of Personnel Forms and Record.* New York: American Management Association, 1949.

Broaded, Charley H., *Essentials of Management for Supervisors.* New York: Harper & Brothers, 1947.

Douglass, Paul F., *Communication through Reports.* New York: Prentice-Hall, 1956.

Improving the Total Program of Your Church: A Guide for Studying and Bettering the Work of Local Churches. National Council of the Churches of Christ in the United States of America (Division of Christian Education, 79 East Adams Street, Chicago 2, Ill., 1954 [Ninth Printing]). This guide was developed co-operatively by Protestant Evangelical forces in the United States and Canada through the International Council of Religious Education.

Kelley, Earl C., *The Workshop Way of Learning.* New York: Harper & Brothers, 1951.

Thelen, Herbert A., *Dynamics of Groups at Work.* Chicago: University of Chicago Press, 1954, especially pages 128-217.

MATERIALS

Any church will find the expense a wise investment to acquire prefabricated components for making organization and flow charts, including a chart board. Such materials may be obtained from CHART-PAK, Inc., 104 Lincoln Avenue, Stamford, Conn.

In this chapter the author has deliberately avoided giving *forms,* since these should be worked out by each church to meet its own particular needs. The references given in this bibliography, however, are adequate to guide any group in the development of its own forms and charts.

The basic control card in the church operated as a group workshop is the individual, cumulative role record. In the administrative catalog of the church there should be a role record of every man, woman, and child related to the church in any way. This role record should give the name, address, telephone number, age, education, special interests, aptitudes, and skills, together with the cumulative performance record of work in the life of the church. The administrator's task is to see that each person in the catalog regularly has opportunities opened to him for involvement, participation, and performance in such a way as to challenge the best that is within him, provide him with an incentive for personal growth, and lead to that deep spiritual satisfaction which comes from heartfelt activity in worth-while achievement.

PART II

Dynamics of Spiritual Growth in Groups

7.

*Developing Solutions Through
Group Discussion:*

THE FACE-TO-FACE GROUP

The power center and growth-stimulating arena of every group
operation lies in the face-to-face discussion of a problem carried on by members in a meeting. In the pooling of information, in the sharing of experiences and ideas, "people working
together with people" generate energy and competences which
range from the capacity of any one member to the total resources of all the members added together—plus something
more. Discussion in a group as a process of exploring, sharing, learning, discovering, doing, and growing—the habit of
talking things over—produces a healthy climate of involvement, participation, and teamwork. The moments of face-to-
face discussion provide an opportunity for social and spiritual
development. The interstimulation that occurs as the group
works through its problem produces a "multiplying factor"
which makes the total production and change a new value. By
discussion in a group meeting, the strength of each member
can be multiplied by the strengths of all the others.

Figure 8 visualizes how discussion multiplies results. In the
beginning each member around the table differs from every
other—in life history, in physical appearance, in capabilities
and skills, in education, in vital interests, and in many other
respects. Each person looks at that part of the problem which
interests him from his own frame of reference and in terms of
his own experience and outlook. In the interplay of conversation the facts each member knows and the opinions he holds
collide with those of other members. Because of this very wide
difference among the persons around the table, the group has
the varied resources necessary to explore the problem thor-

Figure 8.

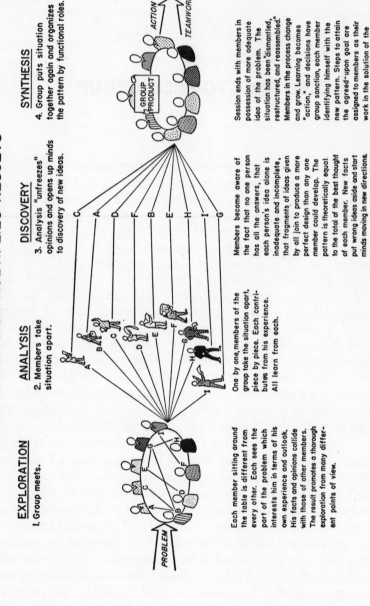

HOW DISCUSSION MULTIPLIES RESULTS

EXPLORATION
1. Group meets.

Each member sitting around the table is different from every other. Each sees the part of the problem which interests him in terms of his own experience and outlook. His facts and opinions collide with those of other members. The result promotes a thorough exploration from many different points of view.

ANALYSIS
2. Members take situation apart.

One by one, members of the group take the situation apart, piece by piece. Each contributes from his experience. All learn from each.

DISCOVERY
3. Analysis "unfreezes" opinions and opens up minds to discovery of new ideas.

Members become aware of the fact that no one person has all the answers, that each person's idea alone is inadequate and incomplete, that fragments of ideas given by all join to produce a more perfect design than any one member could develop. The pattern is theoretically equal to the total of the best thought of each member. New facts put wrong ideas aside and start minds moving in new directions.

SYNTHESIS
4. Group puts situation together again and organizes the pattern by functional roles.

Session ends with members in possession of more adequate idea of the problem. The situation has been "dismantled, restructured, and reassembled." Members in the process change and grow. Learning becomes "action," and decisions have group sanction, each member identifying himself with the new pattern. Steps to attain the agreed-upon goal are assigned to members as their work in the solution of the problem.

oughly from many different points of view. The fact that there is heterogeneity in the beginning makes possible a sound homogeneity in the end. Segment by segment the members attack the problem. They take the situation apart. Each person contributes from his experience; all learn from each. By patience, objectivity, and analytical insight the group "unfreezes" the opinions initially held by the members. The honest discussion opens up minds to the discovery of new ideas. Members become aware of the fact that no one person has all the answers, that each person's idea alone is inadequate and incomplete, that fragments of ideas contributed by all join together to produce a more perfect design than any one member could develop by himself. New facts and points of view set wrong ideas right and start minds moving in new directions. Out of the process and discovery emerges a synthesis. The group formulates a solution to the problem which faces reality and which is adequate to the situation. Decisions arrived at and goals established have the sanction of group acceptance. Steps to attain agreed-upon goals are assigned to members as task roles. The outcome of the group work moves forward as action teamwork to achieve a purpose. Many-sided change takes place in the group process. Around the table people "thaw out" their personal rigid conceptions, develop a working pattern that evolves from the contributions of all, and organize this pattern into a new and better consensus through interaction and interpersuasion.

In the language of group dynamics there are two basic concepts which are important in developing the maximum productivity of the group and in providing for the individual growth of its members. The first of these, to repeat the discussion in Chapter 1, is *involvement*. The second is *participation*. Involvement, it will be remembered, means the process by which the experience, skill, and wholehearted interest of individual people are tied into the planning and doing of a common task. Participation means the sharing of responsibilities so that each person "involved" contributes his best because he feels himself to be a useful and necessary part of the activity. By encouraging the "best" performance of the "most" people, the group becomes democratic and productive.

In any democratic operation which places value on the

"growth of persons," people must be entrusted always with more responsibility than they are at the moment fitted by experience to bear, as a condition of their development. At the Tavistock Institute in London, specialists often speak of the human being in the figure of speech of an "iceberg." By this they mean that a large part of the person, like an iceberg, is submerged and therefore inaccessible to communication. A group process is dynamic when it lifts the underwater part of the human "iceberg" to the surface to permit the exposure of the "whole person." The church operating as a group workshop proposes to deal with the whole human being.

To be genuinely productive, a group must function within the context of certain fundamental conditions. First of all, the group must be free. A group is free when its members come together without anxiety, ready to take part and to participate in the discussion without any uneasiness prompted by fear of consequences which may come from an objective expression of ideas. Second, the members must be participant—ready, that is to say; they must be prepared to enter into the give-and-take by which ideas are forged. Third, members must have accurate information available—reliable facts on which thinking can be based. Fourth, the members must possess a sense of responsibility, that is, they must feel that the consequences of their actions will hold them accountable for the wisdom, integrity, soundness, and rightness of their decisions. Fifth, the members must share a readiness, as the British say, "to work the problem through," that is, to stick to the task even when the going gets rough. When a group environment provides these five conditions, it has laid out the playing field for productive group work.

Productive work in discussion in face-to-face groups results from "positive behavior" in a meeting. A meeting moves through six phases: the approach; the drawing out; input; feedback; acceptance; and summation. Each of these terms requires explanation.

The *approach* refers to the way in which the leader makes his contact with the group in presenting the problem at issue. The character of the approach tends to determine the climate in which the group will subsequently operate. The effective leader does not confront his group with a cut-and-dried, rig-

idly defined agenda. Rather, he explores *with* the members
their ideas about ways to attack the problem. In this process of
exploration, the group relaxes. Its members develop confidence
and mutual respect. They "find themselves." The healthy emotional climate of involvement and participation thus created
releases energies. There is freedom to think, freedom to feel,
and freedom to express. From the beginning of the session the
members of the group are engaged in a common effort to find
the right and one best way to move forward. In a group so led,
as Professor Nathaniel Cantor, of the University of Buffalo,
says,

> A person can face himself, assume responsibility for
> thoughtful choices and decisions, recognize his weak-
> nesses, use his strengths without defensively imposing
> them on others, and accept help from others. In the free
> and open exchange of ideas and feelings between the
> members of the group, no one needs to be competitive,
> no one has to win or prove himself right, no one has to
> be exposed to ridicule, sarcasm, or condemnation. To-
> gether the members explore ideas or situations, test their
> insights, old and new, through the combined contributions
> and helpful criticisms of all the members and the leader.
> Feeling the support of others, recognizing the common
> failings and uncertainties of all, being understood, being
> left free to make their own decisions, being respected for
> their unique contributions—these attitudes and feelings
> about standards lead members of a group to such a co-
> operative atmosphere that no individual feels isolated,
> unsure of himself, hostile, competitive, or defensive. He
> can be himself.[1]

The approach is a "warming up" period during which the
leader encourages participation to create a congenial emotional climate. The leader introduces himself to the members
whom he does not know, sees that members are introduced to
one another. Sometimes this is done before the meeting begins. At other times the leader may ask each member in turn
around the table, at an early point in the agenda, to introduce
himself. When the group has an idea about the people who
compose it, the time has come for a caucus of ideas. By again
asking each member in turn around the table, the leader

provides the opportunity for every person to say something early in the meeting. It may be a comment on some preliminary problem that has tentatively been brought to the table. Sometimes members make observations from their own experiences. Sometimes the blackboard is used to inventory ideas brought up by members, to find out how widely their ideas vary and how much agreement exists. Sometimes a resource person or film places a common experience before the group from which the members can take their point of departure. The importance of the approach is merely to provide an opening so that members feel that the meeting is "theirs," that they are necessary parts of the operation, that they are "in the act," that they count, are wanted and respected.

Having developed an approach, the leader next proceeds to a *drawing out*. Just as a bottle opener takes the cap off a bottle, so skillful questioning serves as a useful way to break down the reserve of members, to unlock their inhibitions, and to draw each one out and into the active movement of the discussion. In fact this drawing out is the task of all the mature members of the group, not just the leader. Individual members direct leading questions to other members. Certain members are asked to read documents, letters, and other material. The leader may invite some member to summarize. Experienced group members become as sensitive to the process of involvement-participation as the leader himself. Like the leader, they too want to get the "best from the most."

Like a factory, a group requires raw materials to work upon. Discussion must be enriched by the best thought and experience which can be brought to bear upon the problem at hand. The output of any group will depend upon the quality of the *input*—the facts, ideas, skills, and energy that flow through members into the group discussion. Some members will introduce carefully prepared memorandums. Such written documents supply a solid contribution. Resource specialists and materials may be presented. No group wants to arrive at decisions which are accepted because they are the easiest, or evoke the least opposition, or are supported by the "right" people with the greatest prestige or power to persuade. The input provides fresh, authoritative information as "raw materials" for processing in the group workshop.

Quite as important as input is *feedback*. This is a term brought into group dynamics from the field of engineering. Technically it means that a part of the output of a machine is returned as input at a proper time. It means that production information is channeled back to members. This feedback takes a number of different forms. Sometimes it may be in the nature of reports. At other times it may deal with qualitative evaluation of the productivity of the group. How far has the group moved toward the achievement of its task goal? Feedback of this character is a critique, an appraisal of the group activities and the work of its members—much like a schoolboy's report card. The critique points out how much and how well the work is being done.

All the while, the group is moving toward a stage in its deliberations known as *acceptance*. As the group discusses a subject, a consensus achieved by interpersuasion evolves to the point where it can be crystallized and tentatively stated. By blocking out areas of agreement, by statement and restatement, the group moves toward an agreed position. It is toward this acceptance that the whole group works; its achievement as a result of full participation is the leader's objective.

The final step in the group process is called the *summation*. This is the point at which the actions of the group are tied together. This end step is really a review and explanation of action taken. It should be brief, accurate, and clear. If there have been differences of opinion, the respective positions should be clearly stated and fairly represented.

Ways to Stimulate Group Alertness

Mere wishful thinking does not produce effective participant groups; they result rather from skillful and sincere leadership. There are a number of ways in which the leader can encourage group alertness by providing "listening" and "questioning" roles. *The group experience is really an activity of communication.* Effective communication comes from (1) speaking, (2) listening, and (3) questioning.

Members of any group differ widely in personal backgrounds and experiences. Some hear more distinctly than others. Some associate ideas into different patterns of meaning. Minds wander, so that some listeners may miss important parts of a presentation and obtain incomplete or inaccurate impressions. Different people absorb information at different rates. "He talked too fast," one person will comment. "He bored me, he went too slow," another will observe. "He was too deep for me," still another will confess. Again, the speaker's mind may not move along the lines familiar to the group. "I sure couldn't follow him," some will admit. What each listener hears and remembers is to a large extent the result of his own interests, experiences, needs, and preparation. If the real purpose of a meeting is communication, then it is important to see that ideas get into the heads and hearts of the members of the group—accurately. How much of an idea has "gone across"? What problems related to it have come into the minds of the people as the presentation has proceeded? What points need to be cleared up before people can put the information to work? The process of listening-questioning clarifies ideas by bumping mind against mind until understanding is achieved.

Within the orbit of this major purpose the listening-questioning operation achieves other ends. For example, it

1. Introduces an atmosphere of relaxation and participation.
2. Shows how much of the presentation has been heard, understood, remembered, and applied.
3. Uncovers gaps in the presentation that need to be filled in by further information and explanation.
4. Focuses attention on fundamental points that relate to the specific needs and concerns of the people present.
5. Explores particular angles of application about which the speaker may not be fully aware.
6. Provides opportunity to thrash over ideas as an effective means to test how much of the discussion members have made their own.
7. Gives an occasion to re-examine main points, to summarize, and to tie together the various points of view brought up by questions.
8. Points out what kind of further help the listeners would like.
9. Opens up opportunity for receiving specific recommendations.

10. Helps program planners to discover what topics really interest people, so that future meetings can profit by their reactions.

11. Points out emotional reactions of people—their likes, dislikes, apathies, prejudices, hostilities, and ignorances.

A number of techniques can be used to mobilize the resources of a group for active participation through critical listening. These techniques include overview questions; briefing; listening outline; listening sentinel; listening team; question poser; critique member; action panel; interview; panel segment; after-meeting circle; role-playing interlude; and the buzz group.

The *overview question* technique merely means that at the opening of a discussion a series of questions are stated for which group members should be on the lookout to find answers in the flow of the meeting. Such questions may be put on the chalkboard, circulated as a worksheet, or flashed on a screen. They can be stated orally to the group by a specially qualified person in such order that the questions as announced place in outline order the ideas which listeners may expect. Such questions become hooks for the mind to hang new ideas on as they are presented. If "pointed questions" are tailored-to-order by planning with a speaker in advance of his presentation, they tie together with his presentation and alert the group members to an attitude of attention, expectancy, and discovery.

Another technique, helpful in encouraging critical listening and active participation, is *briefing*. This process involves a short explanation of the purpose of the presentation made to the group and advance tips on what to listen for. Often sample questions can be worked into the briefing statement.

A third technique is the *listening outline*. This may be placed on the chalkboard or distributed as a worksheet to help members recognize the important items.

A fourth technique is the appointment of a *listening sentinel*. As each topic is taken up, the leader appoints one member of the group to have a special responsibility for monitoring the presentation or phase of the discussion. Upon the completion of the topic, the sentinel makes a brief restatement of the presentation. If it seems desirable to have more than one member monitor the topic, then the listening sentinel becomes "plural" and may be referred to as a *listening team*.

The listening-sentinel role is sometimes expanded into a team function. The team is composed of three members. Member One listens and restates the substance of the discussion. Member Two listens critically and formulates questions which he directs to the speaker to clarify and apply the presentation. He is the *question poser*. Member Three completes the teamwork by summarizing both the substance of the discussion of the topic and the outcome of the questioning. He sums up and applies production experience to the forward task of the group. He gives the *critique*.

Again, a listening panel may provide the means for encouraging participation. The leader divides the group by sides of the table or sections of the room. Each team is given a role to listen for some particular thing. One segment of the group may listen for "points that require clarification." A second segment may be on the lookout for "things we ought to do something about." At the conclusion of the discussion of the topic, the responses of the "panels" bring functional reactions to the clarification and application of the subject.

By designating some members of the group as an *action panel*, the leader provides a means by which the group can have a feedback of specific suggestions for putting the ideas to work.

Still another means of stimulating participation for purpose of clarification is the *interview*. A member, acting like a newspaper reporter, seeks to dig out information and points of view by a series of interrogations. When the "interview" point in the meeting is reached, the leader turns the floor over to the interviewer who proceeds to ask his questions and "develop" his story. Then this member can report back to the whole group, which has witnessed the interview, by way of clarification and summation in the forward action of the group process.

Again, the leaders may appoint a few members to serve as a *panel segment*. These members physically flank the speaker as in ordinary panel pattern. When the topic has been completed, the panel members proceed to discuss the issues raised in the topic presentation.

Then there is the *after-meeting circle*. Always there are people who are especially interested or especially confused. Both groups want to go into the topic in greater detail. Provision for after-meeting informal discussion can be of enormous value to certain members of the group.

Role playing has become so much a part of the group process that it deserves special treatment. Actually role playing is a way of introducing ideas, points of view, and emotional positions into a discussion. Essentially this technique represents an unrehearsed acting out of situations which confront the members of a group. In an informal, lively, and dramatic way, members act out real life situations without real life punishment for consequences. The technique encourages participation, clarifies positions, and resolves difficulties. Role playing can be used as a training device quite as well as a means for working through difficulties. Role playing enacts a dramatic situation. It has plot—a problem with beginning, crisis, and denouement. It provides suspense. It is vivid and interest-commanding.

Role playing has many uses in productive group work. Five of the most important of these are: to develop involvement as a point of departure in getting the meeting in motion to command interest, and to create a climate of warmth; to pose a specific problem to provide input so that group members have a common situation to face; to test out alternative ways of dealing with the problem before the group; to develop a sensitive awareness to the issue at hand; and to work through difficulties which arise in the course of the group process.[2]

Like role playing, the *buzz session* has found a useful place in group technology. Often it is used to the great benefit of the group process; and often it is much abused to the detriment of the group operation. Any technique is valuable only at the point where it helps the group to produce. A buzz session, set up merely because buzz sessions are currently fashionable, often wastes time and annoys sensible people. The technique was originally developed as a means of breaking up a large audience into small and intimate conversational groups so that they could probe into a question. Actually the process has been used for ages in the Orient, where people cluster in little groups to get a consensus of understanding before they speak out. At any rate, the buzz group has a generally accepted pattern. In size it includes about six members —although the need for intimacy overrides arbitrary numbers. In duration the buzz group may last six minutes—although the need to talk the topic through overrides arbitrary time limitations.

Thelen states a few principles which contribute to buzz-group success in moving the group in the direction of purposeful activity:

1. The larger group "must be instructed very clearly about (a) what it is to discuss, (b) what and how it is to report back to the total group;" (c) how it is to break into the buzz group; and (d) how it is to reassemble.
2. The audience should be "given good reasons" for decentralizing the discussion into the smaller groups.
3. The leader should terminate the buzz work period when productivity and interest seem to be ebbing, by giving a two-minute warning.
4. Upon the reassembly of the whole group, the subgroups report back.[3]

Thelen inventories four situations in which the buzz-group technique is especially valuable:

1. To get a meeting started on significant problems, with the members assuming considerable responsibility.
2. To set up the agenda for a meaningful learning experience.
3. To overcome a feeling of helplessness or apathy or to redirect a group toward action.
4. To test a set of ideas, and to increase communication between speaker and audience.[4]

WAYS OF RESOLVING GROUP DIFFICULTIES

As groups work through their problems, members sometimes find themselves in sessions which seem to be blocked by impasses from which there seems no way out. The group begins to flounder. It wastes time. Members become bored, fidgety, and irritable. The group moves into a climate of tension and strain. In moments of this kind the leader finds his largest opportunity to help the group mature its participant skills and to encourage spiritual growth. He needs to introduce some new factor.

He may make use of a number of techniques to restore group productivity. Such techniques may include the caucus; the buzz session; role playing; the tête-à-tête; resource input; silence; recess; and goal review. Each of these techniques requires brief explanation.

The *caucus* is a very simple device designed to draw out the ideas, opinions, and reactions of each member by the simple process of asking each member of the group in turn to state his reactions. This is an effective technique because it provides for total, immediate, and orderly participation. In the process of the circuit around the table, ideas are clarified, new angles are brought forward, and all the members can see what the general consensus of the members is.

The *buzz session* is merely declaring an intermission of a few minutes during which members in small groups of perhaps six talk about the point at issue. In the process of relaxation and conversation, some new factor enters the situation. When members begin to discuss the subject in the reconvened meeting, they report their thinking. The meeting begins to "move" again.

Likewise, *role playing* may be helpful in working through periods of difficulty. In this kind of role-playing situation the leader says to himself: "Now, let's stop right here a moment. Let's put this issue before us by dramatic analysis. Let's pretend. Let's trade places. Let's see how this issue looks when we stand on the other side of the fence. How would this problem look if you were in my place?" In stress role-playing interaction, members assume the roles of key persons. They behave as they think the person who actually occupies that role would behave under the circumstances. Used within the context of the discussion, role playing operates something like this. The leader says: "Let's take a look at this situation from a different point of view. Suppose, Mr. X, that you transform yourself into Mr. Y, and that Mr. Y becomes Mr. X. Let's see how you in these assumed roles would work out this issue. Having exchanged places, the two men, with accurate but dramatic performance, proceed to put forward their respective points of view. Out of the informal and extemporaneous drama comes a new perspective, a mutuality of understanding. Then the group resumes its productivity. Leaders use this device with caution and only employ it where the stress will not be disastrous.

The *tête-à-tête* represents an entirely different type of technique. Occasionally in a meeting apparently irreconcilable differences will arise, especially among a few persons and often in relation to the use of words in documents which the group is considering. No amount of argument seems to resolve the difficulty. Indeed, the issue begins to consume the time of the whole group beyond its real worth. Under such circumstances the leader can excuse two or more members from the meeting, to retire to another room. In intimate and direct discussion these members find common ground and report back to the group. Again the meeting begins to "move."

Another method of breaking deadlocks in meetings is the provision for *resource input*. By this technique some person of acknowledged competence is brought into the group to present facts, opinions, to comment on positions held by various group members, and to evaluate the work of the group at a particular point.

The period of *silence* provides an effective method for letting time act as a therapy. Silence permits what the Quakers refer to as the "Inward Light" to act upon "personal experience within the fellowship." It instructs and transforms the conscience as the true guide of life.

John R. Mott, who was a great master of group leadership, often called a *recess* when the group ceased to produce. "Many times," Mott told the writer, "I have said frankly to people in a meeting: 'Brethren, we are getting nowhere.' At such points when we were apt to flounder and get on one another's nerves as a substitute for getting ahead with the work at hand, I have recessed meetings for intercession and meditation. During the recess the group members relax, gather in natural huddles, and return with clarified points of view and readiness to get on with the work again."

Finally, *goal review* provides a direct method by which the attention of the whole group is refocused on its purpose and the progress or lack of progress that has been made.

In developing solutions through group discussion, the leader demonstrates his competence to the extent that by change of methods and change of pace he can maintain conditions of good productivity.

Readings

Adult Leadership, issues September, 1952, through June, 1953.

Cantor, Nathaniel F., *Dynamics of Learning.* Buffalo: Foster & Stewart, 1950.

Chase, Stewart, *The Power of Words.* New York: Harcourt, Brace & Company, 1954.

Hall, D. M., *The Dynamics of Group Discussion.* Danville: Interstate, 1948.

Smiddy, Harold F., *Integrating and Motivating for Effective Performance* (booklet). New York: General Electric Company, 1955.

Strauss, Bert and Frances, *New Ways to Better Meetings.* New York: Viking Press, 1951.

Thelen, Herbert A., *The Dynamics of Groups at Work.* Chicago: University of Chicago Press, 1954.

Utterbach, William E., *Group Thinking and Conference Leadership.* New York: Rinehart & Company, 1950; and *Decision through Discussion* (booklet). Columbus: Ohio State University, 1948.

8.

Maturing Group Skills:

TECHNIQUES OF PARTICIPATION

The quality and the tempo of change produced in the group process depend to a large extent upon the maturity of the participant skills of the group members. These group skills can be developed and perfected by good coaching, practice, and performance in the same way that a pianist masters his instrument, the swimmer his stroke, and the golfer his drive.

MATURE CONFERENCE TYPES

Around every table a mature conference group must have members who act functionally. Figure 9 identifies ten of these mature participant roles.

Perhaps the most important skill to be acquired by a mature group participant is that of *catalyst*. A catalyst seeks continually to involve all the group members in "thinking through" the problem at hand. He wants to get the reactions and the contributions of each member—to draw everybody out and into the thinking. He wants to get the team warmed up for the game. The catalyst is a role every member needs to play; the role runs through the whole meeting from beginning to end. Substantially, it represents a sincere determination to give one's best and to bring out the best in others. The catalyst speeds up the process of group interaction and interpersuasion.

A second role is that of the *proposer*. To get the group into action, some member must make a proposal; somebody must initiate. The proposal is the push which starts the group engine running. While the proposal may seem very clear, obvious, and necessary to the member who initiates it, it will doubtless appear novel, vague, and complicated to the mem-

Figure 9.

ROLES IN MATURE CONFERENCE GROUP

Functional participant skills encourage each member to give his best and bring out the best in others.

The *Catalyst* speeds up the process of productive interaction.

— — — — — — — — — — In the course of a meeting the same member may assume all the conference roles. He demonstrates mature skill by his ability to shift roles for the purpose of sustaining the quality output of the group.

bers who have not been thinking about it at all. Charles F. Kettering, the wizard of General Motors Corporation, says that a man can send a message around the world in a fraction of a second but that it takes many years to get an idea through a quarter of an inch of a man's skull. The proposal introduced into the group needs to be explained.

A third role, therefore, becomes that of *clarifier*. Just what is this proposal? Members want to be clear about the idea. Members want information. To come to a responsible decision in his own mind, each member owes it to himself and to the group to understand. The clarifier recognizes that the member who has proposed the idea has given the suggestion a great deal of personal thought; he would like to benefit from it. He asks questions which clear up the subject in his own mind. He listens carefully to questions asked by others that raise issues of which he has not thought. He wants to get at the facts. At this point the whole group is acting to clarify, to make the suggestion clear.

Once the proposal is fully understood, the group has the task of determining whether it promotes the objectives of the group. Given the facts, the group raises the question as to how they relate to values. What results may be expected from such a project? Is it within the policy scope and purpose of the group? Does it represent the best use of the efforts and resources of the group and its members? These and many other questions must be weighed. The role of members examining goals in terms of proposals, balancing and measuring outcomes, may be described as that of the *weigher*. Taking all things into consideration, is this the right way to proceed? Group members bounce the proposal around, look at it from all sides, and in relation to all its consequences decide whether it should be accepted.

In this process of examination of the value of the proposal, the weighing function is assisted by the *explorer*. The explorer has the kind of mind which keeps conducting a systematic search into the unknown areas to discover clear, chartered, and reliable ground to be claimed. He opens up new territory, comes up with new information, and places new evidence on the balance scales of the group decision. If there are members of the group who have some special knowledge of a subject and who ought to be in a position to appraise the proposal, he wants to hear from them. If experts have been called in, he proceeds to draw on their resources and to listen to their testimony.

As the discussion proceeds and the consequences of the proposal are generally understood, members will differ in their opinions. In mature groups this difference will be looked upon objectively and considered entirely free from personalities. Members of a mature group want to find the right or the best answer on which the group can agree. The group thus arrives at a point of mediation. Around the table members proceed to iron out differences. The role of the member in this process is called the *mediator*.

As thinking goes on and differences are ironed out, the group begins to find common ground for agreement. It is important for this ground to be "claimed" as soon as it is discovered. Members need to pull the facts and opinions together. The member role at this point may be defined as that of *synthesist*. The member or members playing this role make tentative statements of the emerging consensus. The Quakers call this process discovering the "sense of the meeting." One fruitful way of discovering the consensus is to ask each member in turn around the table his reaction. In this way complete participation is encouraged. At the end of the circuit the synthesist can tie the thinking of the group together into some kind of pattern and describe it briefly. There may be a showing of hands or a circuit of the table again to enable members to say whether they do or do not favor the proposal. There may be exploratory motions and amendments. Whatever devices are used, they all have a single purpose: sincerely to develop the common ground on the basis of which the group is ready and willing to stand and to act.

As the consensus appears, some member must play the role of *formulator*. A spokesman for the group attempts to state precisely and clearly in a formula for the record what the group has agreed upon as a course of action. This statement may be in the form of a motion which is voted on. It may be a statement which members agree expresses the consensus of their opinion.

While the group is thinking what should be done, members

must also consider how it should be done. Some member or members must operate in the role of *programmer*. They must think about a plan to carry out the purposes as agreed upon. They must provide ways to implement policy.

Finally, the group in the church workshop needs a member to act as a *gatekeeper*. The term is used in this discussion in a different context from that commonly employed in group dynamics discussions. In a church group the gatekeeper function is to help the members act in mature ways to achieve spiritual growth in behavior patterns of Christian love.

Now it should be made perfectly clear that no one group member assumes the same mature participant role all the time. A proposer may frequently be acting as a mediator. A clarifier may become a programmer. A weigher may be a formulator. *In the course of a meeting the same member may assume all the mature conference roles.* In fact, the maturity of his participant skill is demonstrated by his ability to shift from one role to another within the context of the group discussion to sustain the quality productivity of the group.

Immature Conference Types

Unfortunately, few if any groups have all members with mature participant skills. Hence in the workshop church there needs to be constant concern over and continual coaching in group skills. One of the great contributions of the church can be its contribution to the development of these skills. The maturing of these skills will contribute much to spiritual growth. What a magnificent contribution the church could make to American life if its people through church meetings acquired mature group skills!

The participant immaturity of group members can be identified by symptoms just as accurately as diseases like measles, mumps, or jaundice can be diagnosed. A mere mention of some of the more common types of immaturity will bring the response: "Oh yes, I recognize that kind of group person!"

One type of difficult group member may be described as the *aggressor*. His self-assertiveness may express itself in a number of different ways. He pushes his way around, often provoking resentment. He may monopolize the floor. He may take credit

for another's contribution. He is irritatingly energetic. He be-
haves in such a way as to stifle the contributions of other
members. He is the opposite of the catalyst. He stiffens the atmosphere in which the group works.

The *babbler* is another immature type. She chatters on,
speaking before she thinks, talking without advancing the subject under discussion, sometimes interrupting, consuming time,
boring other members, and exercising little or no influence in
the discussion.

The *bandwagon jumper* seems to have no mind of his own.
He senses what appears to be the drift of the discussion and
takes the popular side. He climbs aboard and begins to beat
the drums. This kind of member seems incapable of objective exploration. He always wants to be "in on the in." One
legislator explained his position by saying: "I have no desire
to be a dead hero."

Then there is the *belittler,* the kind of person who minimizes
the possibility that the group will achieve anything. The attitude of such a person actually tears down the structure of the
group itself. The belittler hangs on the edges of the group in a
half-hearted sort of way, always critical and seldom constructive.

The *blindfish* is a member perfectly at home with the subject under discussion, but whose eyes fail to see the goals in
relation to the operations necessary to achieve them. He knows
the waters of his "cave" perfectly but he has never seen the
opening to a universe beyond. This kind of person can be
very useful, but it takes great self-restraint and sympathetic
understanding on the part of the more mature members to
work the ideas of the blindfish into the forward movement of
group thinking. Often this kind of member circles around and
in a few minutes is back to the same point he was discussing a
few minutes before.

The *blocker* is still another difficult type. He is one who ob-
structs the progress of the group. Generally he is negative,
carrying resistance beyond the point of reasonable consideration. Like the blindfish, he often returns to a topic after it has
been disposed of by the group.

The *conspirator* is a member who has plans and designs of
his own. These plans do not appear on the surface of the dis-

cussion; they do not relate to the welfare of the group; and they are neither openly stated nor frankly discussed. The conspirator type may appear in any kind of group. Do not forget Judas!

The *distractor* is the member who is always switching away from the idea before the group, to draw its attention to something in a different direction. He seems to find it impossible consistently to follow a line of thought and to help the group move forward.

The *dodger* attempts to avoid taking stands on issues by making sudden shifts in positions. He does not propose to accept responsibility. He is an irritatingly elusive member who can never be pinned down.

The *looker-on* is a spectator on the edge of the group process. He finds it all very interesting and enjoyable, likes to be present, but becomes neither involved nor participant.

The *manipulator* is the kind of member who proposes to "manage" the meeting. He wants to determine outcomes in advance. He thinks that he knows the answers and that his answers should be arrived at by the group.

The *pigeonholer* is the member who wants to put every idea in its proper place where it can be classified according to existing patterns, and perhaps once so filed may never be seen or heard from again.

The *playboy* is a breezy individual who makes it clear that he is not involved in the work of the group. He "horses around," annoys people who are putting their efforts to the task at hand, and by a general attitude of indifference makes goals seem silly and proposals to reach them irrelevant in terms of his own important position.

The *pleader* is the person who speaks up for a cause. He ties his reactions into emotional knots, one-sided points of view, and expresses his thought in stereotyped words and patterns. He is concerned with a race or a color or an economic group or an ideology. He is for youth or young married people or senior citizens or veterans. The point is that the pleader approaches the discussion with a closed mind that runs on a one-way track. Every reaction seems to relate itself to his pet position and special interest.

Then there is the *recognition seeker*, the member who uses

the discussion forum to call attention to himself, what he is and has done, and in what weighty light he should be looked upon by the various members.

The *scapegoater* is the member who is forever pinning blame and responsibility for consequences on someone or something as an outlet for hostility and in excuse for what has happened. By his behavior he tries to have the group avoid facing an issue and accepting responsibility for outcomes.

The *sulker* develops a mood which expresses itself in a quiet, self-contained, and peevish resentment toward the group as a whole or toward particular members of it.

The *Trojan horse* is the kind of member who comes to the meeting committed to hidden agenda and to ulterior ends of which the group itself might not approve. The hidden agenda do not show on the surface and unless group members are on their guard, they may be "taken in."

The *wisecracker* takes opportunity to make smart, witty, and often clever comments and asides. While the wisecracker sometimes relieves the tension in a group by causing a good laugh, as a rule he keeps at his specialty so fully that he prevents the group from getting on with its business.

The *wounded* is the sensitive type of member whose feelings are easily hurt. He becomes offended and grieves over injuries sustained within the group.

Of course this catalog of immature types could be shortened or expanded. Only one point here deserves emphasis: immaturity should be recognized so that personal development and group training can help group members to develop more mature participant skills.

X-Ray of Meeting Role Performance

An edited excerpt from the verbatim transcript of a meeting gives a picture of a face-to-face group at work as the members—mature and immature—play their roles:

PROPOSER: The question I wish to raise relates to the wisdom of developing a completely graded church school program for adults. I realize that this suggestion raises a query as to whether we can improve upon our present class organization. I wish to move that we appoint a committee to study this subject and report back to our next monthly meeting.

Those of us who have been thinking about this subject believe that such a graded program for adults will (1) increase the attendance at the church school; (2) provide a desirable service to adults; (3) revitalize adult instruction and interest; (4) deepen the religious understanding and devotional habits of our people.

In short, a graded program for adults will involve more men and women in a more spiritually productive way in the activities of Christian education.

CHAIRMAN: Your proposal is that we appoint a special committee to explore the possibility of developing a completely graded church school program for adults. Do I hear a second to the motion?

BELITTLER: Why?

(The motion was seconded and the discussion proceeded.)

PROPOSER: If I may, I should like to say a word about my motion. Adult interest in Christian education has grown steadily over the years wherever specific provision has been made for it.

Back in 1872 our Southern Baptist Church enrolled 28,765 adults in Sunday school. Today the number has swelled to 2,300,-000 men and women actively engaged in Bible study. This is just the record of our denomination.

Properly to understand the adult Sunday school movement we must look briefly at its history. The adult Sunday school movement originated in 1890. It was based on the idea of having one big class for men and one big class for women. The Baraca-Philathea, or "big class movement" as it was sometimes called, proved one fact: that *adults could be enlisted for Bible study*. Churches awakened to the need.

As the "big class" movement spread, some classes actually became bigger than the morning church congregation. These classes were omnibus affairs. They came to include members of both sexes and all age ranges. But adulthood is not just one uniform status. It is a life cycle, as this chart shows (Figure 10). In each life cycle people have a special life interest. Within this general pattern of adulthood there is need for smaller groupings.

My motion is based on the idea that the time may have come when our church should develop multiple units for the grading of adults. Grading is essentially the plan or process of providing Bible study opportunity for each individual in a class large enough to challenge him and his teacher but small enough to meet his individual spiritual needs. Grading is a practical way of arranging

Figure 10.

SPECIAL INTERESTS IN FOUR STAGES
OF ADULTHOOD CYCLE

PERIOD   PROBLEM

YOUNG ADULTHOOD
SCHOOL TO MARRIAGE

Transition from organized school life, home protection, and adolescent friendships to adult world of life work and individual responsibility. Concern for:

    a. Vocational skill

    b. Advancement

    c. Marriage and own home

MIDDLE YEARS
MARRIAGE TO CHILDREN'S MARRIAGE

Establishment of family and home, prestige status in community, vocational prestige, circle of friendship, development and advancement of children.

FREE YEARS
CHILDREN LEAVING HOME TO RETIREMENT

Interest in children's home and grand-children; general economic security; free time.

SENIOR CITIZENSHIP
FROM RETIREMENT

Engagement in purposeful and happy associations; comfort.

In all periods concern for purpose and meaning of life.

people in classes according to age ranges wide enough to permit growth and narrow enough to be teachable.

The initial step in grading is the assignment of a definite age range to different classes. The final step is the enlistment of adults in the proper classes on the basis of age. Experience has shown that the age span should be about two or three years, and never more than ten. Normally the adult interest spans a ten-year cycle. A wider span increases the difficulty of teaching and makes individual learning less effective.

I wish to point out that grading is only a means to an end. The end is the maximum spiritual development of each individual for whom the church is responsible.

In presenting this summary, I wish to say that I know that the discussion of this proposal will meet with strong emotional reactions. Certainly there are two sides to the question. Nevertheless I do feel that we have an obligation in this committee to consider the plan. It is for this purpose that I have made my motion.

(The discussion proceeded.)

CLARIFIER: Let me see if I understand your proposal. Your idea is to break down the Baraca class into smaller groups based on age ranges.

PROPOSER: Yes, you have summarized my suggestion correctly. By taking such a step, we will interest more people and better serve their spiritual needs.

BANDWAGON JUMPER: Sounds good to me. Let's try something new for a change.

BLINDFISH: What's wrong with our present organization? When something is going good, why upset the applecart?

PLAYBOY: As I was saying, Sunday school is the only educational institution people never seem to graduate from. Why not give people a rest and let them listen to the TV?

WEIGHER: Isn't your proposal a reversal of the whole philosophy of the Sunday school movement? Isn't it a right-about-face? I should like to balance the reasons for a change against maintaining our present program.

PROPOSER: The reason why I have suggested the consideration of a graded adult program is because there is reason to believe that such a program will reach more people with greater spiritual effectiveness. I know that we are doing a very good job now, but I think we can do a better one, that's all. We have learned a lot about Christian education in the last century since the organized adult class movement started to roll.

DISTRACTOR: It sounds like a new-fangled idea of the new pastor to me!

MEDIATOR: Maybe he has some ideas that we ought to consider.

BELITTLER: I'll tell you one thing. I know that Will Harris will blow his top and get out of the church if you break up the class he is teaching.

GATEKEEPER: I suppose our standard to judge by here is what kind of adult organization will help people most to find and know God and serve him in their daily lives.

EXPLORER: Am I correct in thinking that the graded adult program would require more teachers?

BELITTLER: Where are you going to get them? Will Harris has been teaching that class for thirty years—and I don't see anybody in line to take his place.

BLINDFISH: It looks to me as if everything is going good now. Why not let well enough alone?

BELITTLER: Is there any reason to break up the class? There were eighty-six out last Sunday. Aren't they satisfied? Aren't they happy? Why disturb us? I'm in the class and I intend to stay in it!

PROPOSER: I would like to answer the question about the need for more teachers. Yes, the graded adult program would require a lot more teachers. I am confident that they can be enlisted and trained.

EXPLORER: One more question. With more classes, would we not require more classroom space?

BELITTLER: Where's the money coming from?

PROPOSER: Yes, we would need more educational space. That is one of the problems for us to think through in relation to the proposal. Personally, I feel that it is encouraging to think that we shall need more space for our growing program.

DODGER: This whole thing is a new idea to me. I want to think through what it implies.

EXPLORER: Let me ask this question for my information. Has this graded adult program been attempted anywhere in our vicinity, and if so, what results have been experienced?

PROPOSER: The answer to your question is that St. Mark's Church graded its adult department last year.

EXPLORER: Just one other question—if I may. How would you divide up the cycle of adulthood by classes?

PROPOSER: In ten-year spans, say 24-34, 35-44, 45-54, 55-64, 65-74, and 75 and up. I think we should study each of these groups to determine their needs and interests. Adults keep growing and their needs keep changing.

BLINDFISH: I don't understand the reason for all this discussion. As John said, there were eighty-six out Sunday. That sounds pretty good to me. No other church in town had that many adults out to Sunday school!

BABBLER: Well, sometimes you have more out, and sometimes less, but there's always a good attendance.

GATEKEEPER: Our real concern is to find the kind of organization that will permit us to understand more fully the love and grace of God.

FORMULATOR: I think the proposal has merit, but if it is handled in the wrong way, it could blow us sky high. What would you all think of inviting to the next meeting of this committee the adult leaders to hear our neighbor, the superintendent of St. Mark's adult division, tell about his experience with multiple units and graded classes for adults?

PROGRAMMER: That seems to me to be a good suggestion. Let's look into the proposal. I move that we invite the St. Mark's superintendent to our next meeting. I make that as an amendment to the motion before us.

SYNTHESIST: What you are suggesting, Harry, is that we examine the experience at St. Mark's as the next step in the study of this proposal?

MEDIATOR: Of course with the understanding that the pastor, superintendent, and adult class officers are here. We want the people involved present when we discuss the subject. I am sure that by the proper approach we can work out whatever is best for the church. Some of us can't absorb these revolutionary ideas all at once.

GATEKEEPER: We have a common purpose. We are trying to find the most effective way to experience God in life.

GROWTH IN MATURE PARTICIPANT SKILLS

An effective group concerns itself with the improvement of participant skills. One of the changes which skill improvement brings about in the person and in the culture of the group is the confidence in the method of contributing to the discussion. Any meeting becomes a practice field for training in group participation. While clinical guidance requires specialized personnel, simple and rewarding training can be conducted by the use of the Participation Profile given in Figure 11. This chart has two scales. The *C scale* at the top inventories some of the chief behavior patterns of members who *contribute* with mature skills to further the group's productivity. The *H scale* shows the extent to which members behave in ways which *hinder* the group's work. By the use of this profile, an observer can plot the behavior pattern of any group member. In the same way any group member, looking objectively at himself, can plot his own pattern. If composite profiles are developed, the resulting chart will show the maturity or immaturity of the total group performance.

If one were asked to express in a single phrase the chief characteristic of mature participant skill, the answer might well be expressed in the words: "the ability to ask 'forwarding' questions and to make 'forwarding' comments." Forwarding questions and comments are simply those personal, positive, and incisive reactions in the group discussion which advance the exploration of the problem at hand. The forwarding attitude tends to make the analysis clean-cut, to bring the alternative choices for action sharply to focus, to identify the hard facts of reality as they affect possible outcomes, to formulate in programmatic ways the emerging consensus of the discussion, and by alert response to help at every point in the economical productivity of the group.

In his important studies at Harvard University, the distinguished sociologist, Professor Pitrim A. Sorokin, defined al-

Figure 11. **PARTICIPATION PROFILE**

INDIVIDUAL ADVANCEMENT OF WORK PRODUCTIVITY OF GROUP

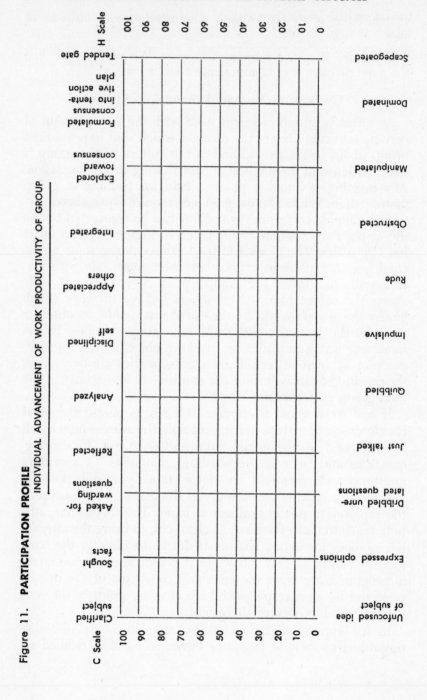

truism as the capacity to share the aims and aspirations of others and to help in their fulfillment. The forwarding attitude represents this kind of behavior within the intimate circle of the problem-centered group. The mature participant seeks at every point in every possible way to accelerate positive change. For himself and for others he tries to help the group to find fulfillment of its aspirations.

Readings

Kelley, Earl C., *The Workshop Way of Learning*. New York: Harper & Brothers, 1951.

Strauss, Bert and Frances, *New Ways to Better Meetings*. New York: Viking Press, 1951.

Thelen, Herbert A., *Dynamics of Groups at Work*. Chicago: University of Chicago Press, 1954, especially pp. 128–217.

9.

Providing Leadership That Catalyzes Change:

THE RESPONSIBLE MISSION

A group tends to take on the quality its leadership communicates. The quality of leadership tends to determine the behavior responses of members. The interaction of group and leadership tends to determine the amount of productivity and the amount of growth which participant individuals experience.

Thelen says concisely that "leadership is the set of functions through which the group co-ordinates the efforts of individuals. These efforts must result in satisfaction to the participants as well as in helping the group in meeting its purposes."[1] Hemphill defines leadership as "the behavior of an individual directing group activities." He says that "the adequacy of leadership is an evaluation of the correspondence between the individual's behavior and the behavior demanded by the situation. . . . A leader's most important function in the dynamics of group behavior may well be that of maintaining group membership as a satisfying experience for the members of the group and facilitating their acting as a unit rather than as separate individuals."[2]

The leader may be described as the most responsible member of a purposeful group. His responsibility may be summarized as an obligation (1) to encourage behaviors on the part of members that advance the purpose of the group; (2) to discover and co-ordinate the widely varied member resources in working out the solution to the problem before the group; (3) to provide role satisfaction through involvement and participation; (4) to set up and utilize technologies which will facilitate the common effort and mutual growth; and (5) to help members develop more mature participant skills. The

124

leader serves as a catalyst. His function is to facilitate production and growth.

John R. Mott observed to the writer:

> Over the years I have led meetings attended by people with deep-seated differences based not only on diverse opinions on policy and practices, but on cultural heritage as well. In all my meetings I have always sought one goal: to achieve the maximum expression of the most points of view by the best voices on the subject—without rancor. Only by such means could we explore an issue to the bottom. All my life I have continued to experiment with the spiritual and psychological techniques of group leadership. I have come to two conclusions: there must always be (1) courteous but drastic thoroughness in exploration and (2) great patience in letting the group talk its problems through. A presiding officer should keep his own views in the background. He should give all points of view a fair and adequate chance of expression. The same man cannot be simultaneously a debater and a chairman.

Harold F. Smiddy, a vice-president of General Electric Company, says that true leadership

> is found in attaining accomplishment of common purposes . . . by participation and persuasion rather than by command. It is, in essence, the interpretation and unification of the aims and activities of individuals and groups in order to ensure mutual and voluntary co-operation, teamwork, and self-disciplined unity of effort toward common goals.[3]

A leader's "size" to a large extent is determined by his attitude toward "opposition" and "conflict." Mary Parker Follett used to point out that since men cannot avoid conflict, they should use it. Rather than condemn it, they should set it to work. When two desires have been integrated, a solution develops which finds a place for the best in both. Settlement of conflict by domination gives a victory to one side. Compromise means giving up something, but integration develops a new strength out of previous divergencies.

To visualize how conflict may be utilized creatively, Figure

Figure 12.

USING CONFLICT CREATIVELY
How Integration Develops New Strengths Out Of Previous Divergencies

WAYS OF USING CONFLICT

METHOD OF SETTLEMENT

1. DOMINATION

KIND OF PRODUCTION

Victory to one side, defeat to the other; often resentment crystallizing into revenge.

2. ARITHMETIC

Decision by the "numbers racket."

3. COMPROMISE

Each one gives up something he values and trades it for something he can accept.

4. CREATIVE INTEGRATION

Discovery of best in all and multiplication of strength from previous divergencies; all come out with more.

12 compares four different ways of working through situations of difficulty.

The new emphasis on integration does not come from an academic adventure in an ivory tower. It stems from the cold and factual experience of business and industry. In a footnote in a management manual General Electric Company, for instance, points out that a leader acknowledges temporary failure in his task when he substitutes command for persuasion in an emergency, when he, as a professional manager, decides that the temporary use of "command" to "get on with the job" is preferable to continued efforts at persuasion in the particular current situation.[4]

Since skilled leaders are a commodity in short supply, the assurance that group leadership capabilities can be developed is encouraging. Frederick Winslow Taylor, one of the pioneers in the development of scientific management, used to get out of patience with those who were always looking for the ready-made competent man—the man whom someone else has trained. Every healthy group is always developing its leadership.

Four propositions summarize the kind of leadership which encourages productivity and helps members to mature socially and spiritually:

1. A leader stimulates maximum group performance when he distributes the task of leadership among the members of the group.
2. A leader performs his role most adequately when he seems to be most dispensable.
3. A leader's major task, recognizing that he is especially responsible for the group's progress, is "to set and maintain the conditions required for the group's maximum intelligence to assert itself."[5]
4. A leader provides for religious quality when he leads the members to an awareness of Christian values in the definition of group goals and in the interactions of the persons in the group.

THREE LEADERSHIP TYPES

For purposes of this discussion leaders may be classified in three categories: the boss, the overseer, and the catalyst. Each of these types of leadership tends to determine the climate of the group and the participant pattern. The reactions of members to leadership may range from obedience and dependence, as Figure 13 points out, to continuing growth in initiative, the capacity to bear responsibility, and the awareness of values.

When a leader is a *boss*, for example, dictating plans and making decisions, group members tend to become his minions. They work under his orders and await his commands. They act as machines. When the switch is turned on, the people go into motion; when it is pulled, they cease to operate. Group members thus become puppets and automatons. Instead of experiencing growth, individuals wither; instead of discovering and inventing, they acquiesce.

Another type of leader acts as an *overseer* solicitously caring for the welfare of the group. Under this kind of leadership, the members of a group tend to become timid and defenseless, expecting that the leader will always attend to their good. Like slaves serving under the boss, they experience no inner growth. Rather, they are likely to become complacent, unresourceful, unimaginative, acquiescent routineers.

A third kind of leader is the *catalyst*. He encourages participation and reaction. He seeks the kind of group pattern that provides "space" for people to grow in. Under the catalyst type of leadership, people mature as participants. The human power which lies as a potential within the group is released and given direction. The group "multiplier" is put to work. The leader, in the catalyst role, becomes just the one member of the group who bears the heaviest responsibility for seeing to it that all the members work—and work together. Work in this context means wholehearted participation of all the members in the achievement of the common purpose. They are fully involved. They have a stake in the outcome. They are committed.

Catalytic Leadership and Productivity

While bosses and overseers are everywhere present in group life, research indicates that the catalyst-type leader contributes most to productivity, participant satisfaction, and personal growth. Such a leader works to keep the channels of com-

Figure 13.

GROUP PRODUCTIVITY UNDER DIFFERENT
TYPES OF LEADERSHIP

<u>TYPE OF LEADER</u>

<u>CHARACTER OF GROUP
WORK PERFORMED</u>

THE CATALYST
  releases human potential,
  encourages reaction
  and participation _ _ _ _ _ _ _ _ _ _ _ _ _ _ _ _ _→ group members grow in initiative,
  responsibility, productivity, and
  sense of personal worth.

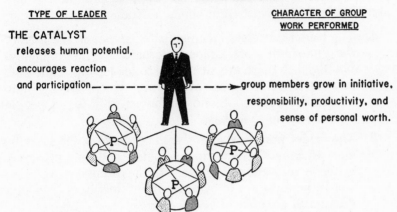

THE OVERSEER
  cares for the details
  of people's welfare
  solicitiously _ _ _ _ _ _ _ _ _ _ _ _ _ _ _ _→ group members become complacent,
  unresourceful, unimaginative,
  acquiescent routineers.

THE BOSS
  dictates plans and
  makes decisions _ _ _ _ _ _ _ _ _ _ _ _ _→ group members tend to become his
  slaves—obedient, dependent,
  often resentful, and frequently
  grumbling clandestinely.

munication open so that all the relevant resources of all the
different people in the group can flow into the meeting. Such
a leader *facilitates change*. He guides and stimulates group
performances toward the achievement of its purposes. A catalytic leader has at least eight characteristics:

1. The leader possesses *technical competence in the area of
    the group's interest*. Colonel Bernard S. Waterman says
    bluntly that there are two parts to leadership: "knowing
    your stuff—or technical proficiency which helps you to
    choose the right goal; and the human skill to get people
    to want to do their best."[6]

2. The leader performs a *gatekeeping function*. He must be
    alert to identify facts, technologies, and sets of agree-
    ments as relevant or irrelevant to the discussion. In other
    words, he must act to evaluate input, feedback, and pro-
    duction in general.

3. The leader maintains the activity of the group as *explora-
    tory, experimental, and free from dogmatic rigidities*. The
    genius of the group activity lies in the thoroughness and
    objectivity with which the members explore the nature
    of their problems and weigh the consequences of alterna-
    tive courses of action. The leader has the responsibility
    for guiding and focusing the exploration in the way most
    adequate to mobilize individual resources to achieve ef-
    ficient progress toward the goal.

4. The leader exercises a power that facilitates the group
    process by attention to the flow of *communication and
    timing*. He pays attention to scheduling resource input.
    He arranges for Mr. X to talk with Mr. Y. He proposes
    buzz sessions. He is sensitive to points where role play-
    ing can be helpful. He can suggest materials to be read,
    points of view to be studied. The catalytic leader's con-
    cern with communication is not for the purpose of
    manipulating or dominating. Rather it comes from the
    sincere desire to make thorough explorations relevant
    to the problem and helpful to group production in creat-
    ing a shared framework of ideas, purposes, and recipro-
    cal relationships. It is this movement toward understand-

ing that forges the individuals into an organic unit. The shared ideas, beliefs, expectations, and aspirations which each group member translates into his own performance produce what Frank appropriately calls an "active dynamic togetherness."[7]

5. The leader has a responsibility for steering the group, especially by rehearsing the consequences that may result from alternative courses of action. His activity may be described as "steering by consequences." A group moves toward a goal by a program of thought and action in a sequence of identifiable steps. Each step is taken by discussing alternative courses of action and selecting the one most advantageous course at that particular choice point or "forking of the roads." Since acts are related in a time sequence, that is, since one step naturally is taken after another, each movement alters the situation in the context of which the next act is performed. Hence the leader, steering by consequences, seeks to develop the most information available about each alternative course of action so that the next step can be planned more wisely. In the evolving pattern of the group consensus, the leader has the obligation to see to it that each acceptance is made by taking into consideration full information and weighing all the consequences.

As the group feels its way ahead, the leader and the group members ask themselves a series of running questions. First, they inquire: "What have we learned about the nature of our problem as we have probed into the consequences of alternative courses of action? What have we learned about reality of our own resources? What have we learned about the realities of the situation external to us? In short, to use a vernacular expression, "What are we up against?" Second, the group looks upon its decision in the light of consequences, in terms of the definition of its own responsibilities as they are defined by the course of action taken. Third, the group faces an emotional situation among its own members and in relation to its own morale. That situation is related to what next step is to be taken. Are the members ready to undertake the next step, fully aware of the consequences attached to such action? Do they feel confident in attacking this next stage of the problem? Do they feel that the objective to be attained is worth the cost of achieving it? In short, as Thelen puts it: "How do people now feel with regard to the challenge of the next step?"[8]

6. The leader must be aware that change produced by the acts of his group have *consequences for other groups as well.* "Consequences," Thelen observes, "ramify like the spreading circular ripples on a pond."[9] Because what Group A does may affect what Group B does or may do, Group A needs to determine what part of its experience should be reported to Group B. Again, Group A should think through how the action of Group B can influence its own work. What resources can Group B supply to Group A to make its exploratory work most effective? Here, it is clear, the workshop group experiences the expanding fact of social interdependence.

7. The leader has a special responsibility for focusing attention on *choice points.* A group comes to attention best in response to formulated questions. These questions identify alternative courses of action. To each course there are attached certain inevitable consequences—"If we do A, then we may expect to face situation B."

8. The leader has an obligation to keep the exploratory work of the group within the facts of *reality.* He does not propose, if he can help it, to let the group discussion become impractical or to base reasoning on hypothetical major premises which are fantastic. He keeps the discussion relevant, focused, and unambiguous.

From his experience around the world in action programs, John R. Mott asserted that mankind's supreme need is for great leaders—leaders who live to the utmost limits of their faith rather than their doubts. He explained:

There are too many mechanical men in life, too many routineers, too many people going through motions for motion's sake. There are too few ready to explore a problem, to think through consequences, to make fearless breaks with precedent. There are too few leaders who live as students of the central strategic factor in the hierarchy of priorities.

In emphasizing the need for training leaders, Mott pointed out what he meant in this way: "You will remember that Samuel Morley asserted that he who does the work is not so profitably employed as he who multiplies the doer." He continued:

> Recruiting, training, the wise use of strong men in strategic roles to achieve great goals—there you have it. And what is the first essential of recruiting? To become alarmed! To awaken to need! To be concerned! Every responsible leader should regard this as incomparably his most important single task: to lay siege to strong personalities. My whole experience has taught me that you cannot command the loyalty of strong men by fractional, casual, and occasional approaches. We stumble and fail in our recruiting because we regard it as a human undertaking. The summons in recruiting is threefold: (1) It is a call to personal discipleship. (2) It is an invitation to undertake a specific task. (3) It is the discovery of the right man to undertake the right role. The rare gift in recruiting is not simply to discover the man, but at the same time to discover hitherto unexplored continents of work and the releasing of the one for the other—the identification of men of talent in order to release them for special work.

John R. Mott had in mind the assignment of men to roles necessary for the achievement of goals that were worthy of their supreme endeavor. Their best was challenged by the greatness of the purpose. He made this final observation:

> One of the common failures in leadership performance lies in a neglect of personal evaluation. Early in my career I made it my obligation to sit down quietly after every meeting and write out a criticism of the session. I needed to learn from each experience so that I could do a better job the next time. I have consistently applied to my own life the same rigid measurement. At the beginning of each year I work out a personal balance sheet. I evaluate my own achievements against goals set up. I inventory my

responsibilities and opportunities for the next twelve months. I allocate my priorities. I define the chief targets of my strategy. This kind of personal control of life is the obligation of the leader.

In the group workshop church the objective is to mature the group skills and build a culture that will sustain high endeavor. In the activity of a group stimulated by the catalytic skill of the leader, members make their positive contributions. "Inside themselves" they feel free and unanxious. At the same time they feel responsible. Moreover, they have the assurance that their personal worth is appreciated and respected. They discover that what they do or fail to do has ramifications throughout the whole web of the interdependent social structure.

COMMUNICATION AND THE LEADERSHIP SKILLS

Fortunately the leadership skills can be cultivated by sharpening the ability to communicate. At the point of the problem under discussion by the group, the leader stands on an advancing frontier. Hence in the exploration of the problem and in choice among courses of action based on the weighing of alternative consequences, he has the task of keeping all channels of communication open. The communication skills—the abilities to read, write, speak, listen, think, and participate—can be and are being developed by study and practice. Outstanding leaders have always studied and practiced these communication skills—the eye for reading and observing, the ear for listening, the mouth for speaking, the hand for writing, the mind for thinking, and the heart for understanding. Good books and work manuals are available for use in communications practice.

Effective communication depends upon the clearness of the concept in the mind of the members of a group; the simplicity and accuracy of the language by which the concept is explained and explored; the diplomacy used in presenting ideas and points of view; the understanding and acceptance of the idea by the members of the group as they deliberate upon it; and the maturity of the culture of the group in terms of its habitual way of dealing with new ideas.

EMERGENCE OF A DYNAMIC GROUP CULTURE

Under the stimulating influence of skilled catalytic leadership, the habitual way in which a group acts changes. The sets of expectations and agreements take new form. The members of the group in their changing culture act with a new confidence. Matured participant interactions accelerate the tempo and quality of exploration, agreement, consensus, and action. The group response becomes, as Frank says, "circular, reciprocal, and creative."[10] Then the mature workshop group becomes an accepted way of life.

The end product of genuine leadership expresses itself in a quality of the culture of a group—co-operative, dynamic, and productive. Participation in work and teamwork in such a climate produces role satisfaction through creative involvement and participation. The working group becomes a responsive, living, adaptable, dynamic unit developing and pursuing common goals. By the openness of its channels of communication to the inflow, circulation, and refinement of enthusiasms, it becomes responsive to change and growth. Within itself such a group generates the resources of continuing imagination, increasing knowledge, and developing skills. Worlds become rich and soul-satisfying when each person at the point of his own performance is encouraged and helped to think his best, speak his best, do his best, and be his best.

Readings

Frank, Lawrence K., *How to Be a Modern Leader*. New York: Association Press, 1954.

Hemphill, John K., *Situational Factors in Leadership*. Columbus: Ohio State University, 1949.

Thelen, Herbert A., *Dynamics of Groups at Work*. Chicago: University of Chicago Press, 1954, especially pp. 245–332.

The following books will be helpful in the development of the communication skills so necessary to competent leadership and group participation:

THINKING

Easton, William H., "Creative Thinking and How to Develop It," *Mechanical Engineering*, August, 1946. Available in reprint.

Stebbing, Susan, *Thinking to Some Purpose*. Hammondsworth: Penguin Books, 1941.

Wallas, Graham, *The Art of Thought*. New York: Harcourt, Brace & Company, 1926.

Young, James W., *A Technique for Producing Ideas*. Chicago: Advertising Publications, 1940.

MEDITATING

Stewart, R. J. J., *A Map of Prayer* (Paternoster Series booklet: 1). London: Burnes Oates & Washburne, 1950.

READING

Reader's Digest, Educational Edition.

Witty, Paul A., *How to Become a Better Reader*. Chicago: Science Research Associates, 1953.

SPEAKING

Bender, James F., *How to Talk Well*. New York: McGraw-Hill Book Company, 1950.

Henneke, Ben C., *Read Aloud Effectively*. New York: Rinehart & Company, 1954.

Lee, Irving J., *How to Talk with People*. New York: Harper & Brothers, 1952.

Muir, Dorothy Erskine, *The Art of Conversation*. London: Odhams Press, 1953.

Parrish, Wayland Maxfield, *Reading Aloud*. New York: Ronald Press Company, 1953.

Phillips, David C., *Oral Communication in Business*. New York: McGraw-Hill Book Company, 1955.

Pigors, Paul, *Effective Communication in Industry*. New York: National Association of Manufacturers, 1949.

WRITING

Cooper, Lane, editor, *The Art of the Writer*. Ithaca: Cornell University Press, 1952, especially "The Philosophy of Style" by Herbert Spencer.

Douglass, Paul F., *Communication through Reports*. New York: Prentice-Hall, 1956.

Flesch, Rudolf, *How to Test Readability*. New York: Harper & Brothers, 1951.

Wolseley, Roland E., editor, *Writing for the Religious Market*. New York: Association Press, 1956.

WORDS FOR TEAMWORK

Chase, Stewart, *The Power of Words*. New York: Harcourt, Brace & Company, 1954.

Hayakawa, S. I., *Language in Thought and Action*. New York: Harcourt, Brace & Company, 1949.

Lee, Irving J., *Language Habits in Human Affairs*. New York: Harper & Brothers, 1941.

PART III | *The Creative Culture of the Group*

Goals and Roles in Spiritual Growth:

THE MAXIMUM STRATEGY

David Livingstone used to say that "the end of the exploration is the beginning of the enterprise." John R. Mott preferred to put the idea like this: "The end of the conference is the beginning of the conquest." The last chapter of this book moves forward as an approach to life.

In our study of the church as a group workshop we began with an operational concept. We started our thinking from an assumption which can be verified in everyday experience: *the role is the social unit of human activity. Human relationships exist in action patterns.* And the action pattern is set in motion by the acceptance of a goal. When people begin to work together to achieve a goal, the whole fabric of their relationship is given design and purpose. Roles becomes functionally interrelated under the force of the objective which people pursue.

As we examined the nature of the human group, we found that this social cluster of human beings is actually an operational powerhouse. In face-to-face association, people pool interests, experience, skills, and expectations in an upward thrust that develops purpose and meaning. We noted that the earmark of mature participant skill lies in a respect for the worth of every man. It is also found on the part of each man in a desire to give his heartfelt best and to encourage others to do the same. Mutual and reciprocal encouragement springs up in a common performance whose drive is toward excellence—excellence in achievement and excellence in the self.

From a searching study into operational dynamics, the giant General Electric Company finds is necessary to recognize the concern for mutual growth as a corporation personnel policy.

141

It writes the specification into job descriptions that each manager is responsible first for his own self-development and second for providing both challenges and opportunities for self-development to all the men whose work he manages. A concern for growth—of the person, of the culture of the group, and of the whole church—becomes an index of the quality of a workshop fellowship as in a healthy climate of purposeful work and teamwork the group defines goals, pursues common objectives, and organizes patterns of roles necessary for their achievement. In daily performances on Main Street and Bye Street, the workaday world becomes rich, creative, and soul-satisfying when each person at the point of his own concern and performance becomes aware of the productive power of the group; for the group in its operational way generates an interstimulating, alert, and competent goodness.

Now looking at our exploration in perspective, we come to two conclusions. First, we see that a mature group exists when its members behave in certain mature ways as they perform their task-roles under the organizing and purposeful discipline of a common goal. The competence necessary for mature group participation can be and ought to be mastered within the fellowship of the church. Such operational technique might well be a required part of every Christian education and training program. Second, we have found that the workshop way of transmuting problems into achievements is both a technique and a culture. The creative culture of the group provides an accepted way of ensemble behavior. In the sustaining fluid of such a culture, people who look at life in terms of continuing purposes will, as a matter of habit, become confident, adaptable, constructive, co-operative, resourceful, and respected. The members of a group with such a culture become human beings who respect one another and who are concerned with mutual personal growth. They take seriously their responsibilities toward God and man.

After an operational training group session one night a choir director, a supper chairman, and a church school superintendent stood discussing the workshop ideas on a street corner outside the church. The director observed that a productive workshop group was much like a choir. He said:

In a choral group each person must make his best contribution without "protruding." He must learn to subordinate his own performance to the ensemble—but without self-effacement. He must sing at his best—without letting his voice stick out. Thus he becomes a good citizen in the community of sound. Often I have found singing voices protruding. I have restudied the singer and discovered that a tenor who becomes conspicuous in his performance may fit in perfectly as a bass. All we needed to do was to recast his role. I think I see what this operational workshop is all about. But like the choir, we will have to rehearse and practice the skills.

"I don't know much about choirs, except that I get a lift from a good choral performance," said the supper chairman.

I was thinking of this workshop group from the kitchen standpoint. It's like mixing an angel cake. It takes a lot of different kinds of ingredients and a lot of skill. You have to measure and sift your sugar and flour. Then you must resift the flour and put in just the right amount of sifted sugar for that moment. Then you must add a teaspoon of salt. Then you must crack the whites of ten eggs, add two tablespoons of water, and whip until the whites are foamy. Then add a teaspoon of cream of tartar, and beat until the whites are stiff but not dry. Next you have to whip in gently a cupful of sifted sugar and fold in a half teaspoon of vanilla and a half teaspoon of almond extract. Finally you fold in gradually, a teaspoon full at a time, the sifted flour mixture, pour the batter into an ungreased nine-inch tube pan, and bake in a slow to moderate oven 325 degrees in temperature for about an hour.

I was thinking of this cake-baking process as I sat in the training class. It takes all the contributions of all the people in the group to produce the right kind of activity. It would be hard to say in the kitchen that the egg whites are more important than the pinch of salt, or that sifting the flour and sugar is more important than the oven temperature. It takes all the ingredients, all the proper conditions, and all the skills to bake a real angel cake. Maybe we have been giving more attention to cake-baking than to our human relationships in groups.

The church school superintendent nodded his head. "I was thinking about the Bible in operational terms," he said.

God became man to operate among us on the streets where we live and to be our companion in dealing with the problems we face. In the New Testament it is rarely the "recognized" person who performed with operational distinction. The performance always seemed to keep developing from new and unexpected persons. So it was in the recruiting of the disciples—fishermen, not members of the great Sanhedrin. It was neither the priest nor the Levite who helped the man on the Jericho Road. It was not a disciple but the boy who brought his lunch that provided the material for the miracle of the feeding of the thousands. It was not the Pharisee but the widow with her mite whom Jesus made immortal in the record. It was Jesus who washed the disciples' feet. The advent star rose to light the cradle of a workingman's babe. It did not come to rest over Herod's palace. It was not Caesar but the Master who gave his life that others might have life more abundantly. The situations of life constantly produce people out of unexpected ranks to perform a service with a selfless motive. It is this kind of discovery in action that interests me. And above all, the discovery that greatness expresses itself at those points in life where you least expect it. That thought makes me conscientiously aware of the importance of the fullest involvement and the deepest participation of every person, not just the expected few.

The choir leader carried forward the thought.

Long since, as our training class has progressed, I have become aware that I myself fall short of the ideal man as I have glimpsed him at work in the groups we have discussed. Yet I have glimpsed that kind of person—and I should like to become like him. I am sure that by individual and group concern—meeting by meeting—I can attempt to develop in that pattern. With your help I propose to grow as a mature participant in the work of groups to which I belong. I shall have a new concern with purposes in which I believe as I work in the company of others to achieve goals to which all of us give our heartfelt allegiance. At least, I have a new vision of the work of a choir director!

Thus the leaven of the training class began to work in continuing informal discussion groups—at each person's level of interest and current performance.

Up to this point we have not concerned ourselves with the kind of problem or with the quality of question that is worthy of the Christian man who has grown in stature as a group participant in the workshop church. Irving Babbitt used to say that Rousseau asked the right questions, but gave the wrong answers. He added, however, that it was no small achievement to recognize the right question. A graduate student at Harvard University once asked then President James B. Conant what might be the characteristic of a good chemist. Dr. Conant replied: "A good chemist is a scientist who knows how to ask the right questions at the right time."

John R. Mott faced the issue as to what problems should concern the Christian. On the basis of his long experience, he stated these rules:

> Act at the point of maximum strategy. Life is too short for any other kind of performance. The urgency of the need is too great for lesser goals. In a life which is lived economically the major issue must always receive the priority. Start toward the strategic goal; then conserve results and take advantage of momentum. Since every meeting serves as a stepping stone to a new level of action, be sure that every gain is built solidly into the foundation from which the next step is taken. Tolerate no wasted action nor squandered resources. And always, always take advantage of momentum to achieve further change. In this way you begin where every man finds himself at the moment; but in continuing growth you move forward on ever advancing frontiers. Thus life becomes one purposeful adventure into new continents of interest and service. It becomes a soul-satisfying if strenuous experience. I have found life so from the occasion when I was sixteen. Among piles of boards in a Postville, Iowa, lumberyard, the Rev. Horace E. Warner in the year 1881 lifted my eyes to new goals. My life became an earnest effort to make every decision in the light of the whole world, from the perspective of the dedicated heart.

Goals and roles in spiritual growth—forged in the purposeful groups of the workshop church—here is an operational method which places the techniques of social science in the service of the ministry.

Readings

Cadman, S. Parkes, *The Parables of Jesus*. Philadelphia: David McKay Company, 1931.

Dobson, James O., *Saint Francis*. New York: Fleming Revell, 1926.

Fisher, Galen M., *John R. Mott: Architect of Co-operation and Unity*. New York: Association Press, 1952.

Frank, Lawrence K., *How to Be a Modern Leader*. New York: Association Press, 1952.

Hemphill, John K., *Situational Factors in Leadership*. Columbus: Ohio State University, 1949.

Laville, Louis, *The Meaning of Holiness*. New York: Pantheon Books, 1954.

Mathews, Basil, *John R. Mott: World Citizen*. New York: Harper & Brothers, 1934.

Meyer, Fr. James, *Social Ideals of St. Francis*. St. Louis: B. Herder Book Company, 1938.

Moffatt, James, translator, *The Holy Bible*. New York: Harper & Brothers, 1926, pp. 1031–1340.

Mott, John R., "Lessons Learned in Forty Years of Work in Helping to Establish and Develop National and International Student Christian Movements," *Student World*, October, 1925, pp. 151–160.

Thelen, Herbert A., *Dynamics of Groups at Work*. Chicago: University of Chicago Press, 1954, especially pp. 245–332.

APPENDIX

I. WAYS OF TEACHING

Fundamental ideas of instruction lie behind each technique. Gilbert Highet says: (1) Make it vivid, (2) make it memorable, (3) make it relevant. He restates by urging (1) clarity, (2) patience, and (3) responsibility. "A good pupil is seldom silent. . . . Anything worth learning takes time to learn and time to teach."[1]

METHOD	PRINCIPLE	SPECIAL USE	DRAWBACKS
Apprenticeship	Learning by doing through association with master craftsman	Personal instruction in special skill for particular job by invitation and association	Technique training; man-to-man relationship limits participation to few persons
Assignment	Individual study to digest information in a text	Necessary task to prepare student	Mere memorization of information does not give genuine understanding
Book Discussion	Systematic reading requires effort of preparation	Coherent content gives all members same information as base for discussion	Book must be inexpensive, substantial, readable, with text easy enough not to discourage slow readers. Reading must not require more than two hours a week
Book Review	One person's summary and interpretation of author's thought	Review keeps members current with important selected new works	Effortless listening gives people glib and superficial acquaintance with the idea
Buzz Group	Demobilization of group into small clusters of participants to give opportunity for expression, reaction, and report back to whole group on specific task question	Time out for every person to state idea, ask questions, think through	Idea likely to be shallow, quickly put together, and disorganized
Debate	Argument of sharply focused questions by pro-and-con representatives	Presentation of both sides of a question with combat spirit	Formal and rigid format; presents two sides, but no other alternatives
Demonstration	Show-how performance	Visualization of process to show how an event occurs or a job is done	Performance limited to particular topic
Discussion	Shared opportunity to exchange ideas	Drawing out ideas from experience of all and developing areas of agreement	Size of group limited; loose organization takes time and patience; requires expert leadership
Drill	Mastery of skill by repetition	Co-ordination in motor skill	Monotony, dullness, lack of challenge and new experience
Forum	Presentation of information followed by questions for clarification	Audience obtains specific information it wants	Formality may check free flow of ideas

METHOD	PRINCIPLE	SPECIAL USE	DRAWBACKS
Group Interview	Opinion given by experts in answer to questions	Competent experience from different angles brought to answer one problem	Session apt to "wander"; requires careful planning and leadership to keep it "on the beam"
Group Reading	Action in concert to give same information to all	Full participation to alert people in covering material	Reading limited to materials in hands of each person
Individual Investigation	Personal inquiry	Immediate approach to experience with provisions for individual initiative	Absence of teamwork
Laboratory	Work and experiment with actual materials	First-hand experience to show result by doing	Consumption of time; skill of manipulation and imagination required
Pageant	Presentation of dramatic scenes to depict a theme	Emotional identification with historical backgrounds or organization relationship	Difficulty in production; expense
Panel	Informal discussions of 4 to 8 persons carried on in front of audience for about fifty minutes, with half hour allotted to audience participation. Summary by chairman ties ideas together	Leisurely examination of issue by representative group	Tendency of some members to monopolize time and ramble from subject
Paper or Thesis	Writing out of ideas	Systematic organization of facts and ideas	Laborious individual performance
Project, Field	Shared investigation of problem	First-hand experience	Time; planning; transportation
Question-Answer	Provocation of response by inquiry	Exploration of preparation and reaction by key interrogators; leading out	Formality; embarrassment; possible dullness
Resource Person	Recognized expert sits with group to feed in experience	Competent ideas made personally available	Selection of right person who will stimulate group
Review and Summary	Tying ideas together to give whole picture	Wrapping up ideas to carry home	Not always sharply focused
Role Playing	Unrehearsed acting out of a situation by group members	Opening way to understanding of feelings, positions, points of view, possible outcomes of change	Skill required to make method organic part of whole teaching process and tie in use with whole program; sometimes artificial

METHOD	PRINCIPLE	SPECIAL USE	DRAWBACKS
Round Table	Educational seminar of small group seated around a table to think through an issue	Informal opportunity to thresh through problems	Often shallow, too congenial, and inbred
Singing	Psychological binding of groups in common theme and purpose	Action operation to get physical and emotional participation—a collateral method	Brevity of time periods in which useful; availability of appropriate materials
Skit	Informal dramatic portrayal of ideas	Action representation which can be imitated	Difficulty of writing or obtaining appropriate skit
Solo Performance: sermon, address, recital, speech	One person's rehearsed presentation	Organized and systematic presentation in specified time	Little participation of audience—except as followers
Speech or Lecture (a) speaker alone (b) speaker-forum (c) speaker-panel	Systematic, organized presentation by expert or popularizer designed appropriately to purpose of meeting, type of audience, and allocation of time	Maximum flow in allotted time when audience prepared in advance and follow-up through further study planned	Speaker may be dull, over head of audience, long-winded
Symposium (a) lecture and symposium (b) debate and symposium (c) symposium panel	Authoritative presentation of different points of view on a subject. Each member (4 or 5) speaks for allotted time on central theme from particular point of view. Questions (oral or written) and discussion follow formal presentation	Presentation of issue and examination from its various angles	Skill of chairman in drawing out and summation, and firmness in following time schedule necessary

II. VISUAL AIDS AVAILABLE FOR GROUP INPUT

AID	USE	ADVANTAGES	DISADVANTAGES	SOURCE OF REFERENCE
Blackboard	Development of ideas; illustration and diagram; chalk talks	Flexibility; ease of group participation in use	Chalk rubs off; hard to preserve; not easily portable	Generally available
Cartoon	Characterization of an idea	Graphic impact of summarized idea, generally with humorous touch	Difficulty in finding appropriate cartoons	Design for occasion; enlargement from newspaper and magazines; cartoon slides and filmstrips
Charts	Systematic presentation of material; points may be covered and strips peeled off as each point discussed	Orderly and sustained impression; possible range—from simple listing of points to complex diagrams	Difficulty in preparation	Design for occasion; commercial supplies
Display	Arrangement of materials to tell a story by attracting and holding attention	Unity of theme by tying in rememberable slogans with visual and emotional appeal	A collateral medium; must catch people as they move around	Design for occasion
Film	Enrichment of experience by visualization and organized presentation of material outside range of immediate individual approach	Impact of visual impression; dramatic movement; emotion; must be introduced and followed by proper teaching plan	Reliance on film as crutch to fill up time; film not always exactly on theme; movie attitude of irresponsibility; cost of equipment	Film Council of America, 600 Davis St., Evanston, Ill.
Filmstrip	Orderly sequence of pictures or "frames" on convenient roll	Simple way to present ideas; recordings often included to interpret images	Availability of strips	Denominational boards; national organizations; Educational Film Strip Guide, H. W. Wilson Company, 950-972 University Ave., New York 52, N. Y.
Flannel Board	Presentation of models to support oral presentation by addition of items in sequence	Provides means of emphasizing points in talk by cumulative symbols to demonstrate a pattern	Not always available; generally must be carried to place where needed	Stationery supply stores
Graphs	Visual communication of statistical data	Summarization of quantitative data for quick understanding	Size and visibility; appropriateness to immediate situation; readability of lettering	Design for occasion; enlargement of graphs from newspapers, magazines, and reports

AID	USE	ADVANTAGES	DISADVANTAGES	SOURCE OF REFERENCE
Map	Relationship of particular factors shown on place or geographic basis	Precise location of what is being talked about; can be combined with charts and pictures	Selection of appropriate maps	C. S. Hammond & Company, 1 East 43rd St., New York 17, N.Y.
Model	Miniature example for exact illustration	Presentation of small but actual object	Difficulty of preparation	Design for occasion
Opaque Projection	Projection of images on screen directly from books or documents without use of slides	Common image for group from materials not otherwise available to whole group	Cost and availability of apparatus	Generally available or can be borrowed
Photographs and Illustrations	Pictorial representation; permanent visual records of local situation	Provision of realistic view	Appropriate views tied in with teaching plan	Select for purpose
Posters	Theme impact at points of movement	Collateral aid in communication	Message sometimes too complicated for quick impression	Selected for purpose
Puppets	Humanized creative portrayal of situations	Dramatization of communication	Difficulty of preparation and manipulation	Design for purpose
Recordings	Professional materials for listening and program enrichment	Gives mature presentation	Requires playing unit; suitability for purpose must be studied	N.B.C. Radio Recording Division, 30 Rockefeller Plaza, New York 20, N.Y.; American Library Association, 520 N. Michigan Ave., Chicago 11, Ill.; Listen & Learn, Inc., 303 Empire Building, Milwaukee 3, Wis.
Slides	Projection of still images; widely used in church to show pictures to visualize material	Wide range of availability; slides can be easily made for local use; materials can be made on typewriter for slide projection	Crutch to fill time	Denominational boards
Visual Charts	Development of one-line headline cards to emphasize points as made	Drives home points as they are made; focuses audience attention	Cards must be developed especially for the purpose	Cards must be individually designed by craftsman

III. CONDITIONS FAVORABLE TO ADULT LEARNING

An adult wants:

FACILITIES

1. Good light—so that he can *see*
2. Good acoustics and distinct speech—so that he can *hear*
3. Correct temperature, ventilation, and restful colors—so that he can be *comfortable*
4. Easy chairs—so that he can *relax*
5. Optimum timing—so that he can *endure*

PRESENTATION

6. A teacher who knows the subject and how to present it—so that he can have *confidence*
7. Orientation—so that he can see where he is starting from, where he is going, and how he is going to get there, i.e., *overview*
8. Pacing—unhurried input so that he can follow and *assimilate*
9. Congenial climate—so that he can feel *at home* and *a part of the show*
10. Participation—so that he can express himself and feel that he is *wanted* in the activity
11. Sense of "getting somewhere"—so that he feels he is growing and *mentally awake*
12. Responsibility—so that he shares in the *management* of the group
13. Activity—so that he *does something*
14. Relevancy—so that what is said relates to his *needs* and has roots in his experience
15. Variety in presentation—so that monotony is broken by *effective surprises*
16. Flexibility in approach—so that *content and tempo can be adjusted to his reach and grasp*

IV. THE ORGANIZATION OF AN INFORMATION AND CONTROL CENTER

A church can build an effective information and control center by use of standard equipment, cards, and indexes. Two Wheeldex card files provide the core. These units occupy 7½" x 14" desk space each. Wheeldex makes both sides of the file card fully visible. The cards can be slipped on or off the file at will. An internal stabilizer automatically holds the unit steady for hand-free reading yet permits free spinning rotation.

The dual unit Wheeldex file provides both a record and cross-reference system. Unit 1 supplies an alphabetical listing and role record of every person related to the church as a member, constituent, prospect, or person who can possibly be helped by the ministry of the church. This file is known as the "Cumulative Role Record." Unit 2 provides a "Role Reservoir" to inventory present and potential roles required to carry out the program of the church, together with the names of persons qualified and interested in occupying these roles.

Dual Cross-Indexed Wheeldex Role-Goal File Control Center of "The Group Workshop Way."

For the average church, Wheeldex Number 1535 meets the need adequately. This unit, costing $56, carries 1,500 cards —which means that the information record enables a church to deal with 1,500 individual names. For larger churches, Wheeldex Number 2504 provides space for 2,500 cards. The second identical unit in the duo-file provides for the Role Reservoir.

For the convenience of churches, Wheeldex supplies the specialized file cards in a size 5" x 3". These are issued in four colors: (1) *buff* for men over 21 or men who are married; (2) *white* for women over 18 or women who are married; (3) *green* for boys under 21 or who are not married; and (4) *salmon* for girls under 18 or who are not married. These color indexes provide a visual classification by sex and age groupings. The cards, designed especially for church file use in a role-goal program, may be obtained for $5.00 a thousand. Wheeldex units and file cards should be ordered from Wheeldex & Simpla Products, Inc., 40 Bank Street, White Plains, New York, or through a local stationer.

CUMULATIVE ROLE RECORD

The data provided for on the Cumulative Role Record cover both sides of the file card as follows:

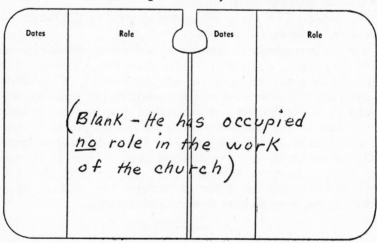

The cell marked "Code" provides space for an entry describing the kind of work performed by the person, as indicated in the *Dictionary of Occupational Titles* described below. The "Family Cross Reference" space at the bottom provides a cell to indicate the family relationships and interrelationships within the church constituency.

On the reverse side, this card provides space for recording, with dates of service, the roles performed by each individual.

ROLE RESERVOIR

The Role Reservoir file inventories all the roles currently available within the church program or which may at some future time become available. In other words, this file is a manpower pool classified by role titles. The code cells in the upper right corner provide space to indicate the job as defined in the *Dictionary of Occupational Titles*. Each Role Reservoir card carries a description of the role *and* the names of persons who are both interested and qualified to perform such a role. The "I" column indicates "interest"; the "E" column indicates experience.

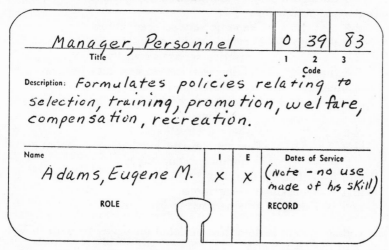

DICTIONARY OF OCCUPATIONAL TITLES

The Dictionary of Occupational Titles, edited by the Division of Occupational Analysis, United States Employment Service, may be purchased from the Superintendent of Documents, Washington 25, D.C. (2 volumes, $7.25). This work is the basic reference tool needed to provide information about occupations and roles. The book catalogs alphabetically and with code numbers the range of jobs in the American economy. By the use of these two volumes, a church can specify how a person earns his living, what training and skills his job requires, and what experience each person brings to the church from his vocation.

OCCUPATIONAL CLASSIFICATION AND CODE

By an occupational classification, the *Dictionary* divides vocations into seven major occupational groups. These, in turn, are divided into smaller groupings at different levels of detail. The seven major occupational groupings are differentiated by the first digit of the code number in this fashion:

0—Professional and managerial occupations
    0-0 through 0-3 Professional occupations
    0-4 through 0-6 Semiprofessional occupations
    0-7 through 0-9 Managerial and official occupations
1—Clerical and sales occupations
    1-0 through 1-4 Clerical and kindred occupations
    1-5 through 1-9 Sales and kindred occupations
2—Service occupations
    2-0   Domestic service occupations
    2-2 through 2-5 Personal service occupations
    2-6   Protective service occupations
    2-8 through 2-9 Building service workers and porters
3—Agricultural, fishery, forestry, and kindred occupations
    3-0 through 3-4 Agricultural, horticultural, and kindred occupations
    3-8   Fishery occupations
    3-9   Forestry (except logging), and hunting and trapping occupations
4 and 5—Skilled occupations
6 and 7—Semiskilled occupations
8 and 9—Unskilled occupations

The coding system is described in detail on pages xix–xxiii in Volume 1 of the *Dictionary*.

EXAMPLES

By reference to the code, a clergyman stands as 0–08.10. This kind of job is defined on page 264 of the *Dictionary*. For purposes of demonstration, assume that a church proposes to develop a functional committee to prepare and maintain the information and control center through the Wheeldex units. Assume further that this committee is to include, preferably, a personnel expert, a specialist in training, and several typists. The personnel expert would be coded 0–39.83; the specialist in training 0–39.87; and the typists 1–37.32.

Take another example. Assume that a church decides to develop a library staff. The personnel committee reviews the Role Reservoir. It finds librarians coded under 1–20.03; library assistants under 1–20.01; public relations officers under 0–06.97; and typists under 1–37.32.

The operation of the information and control center should never become the responsibility of the pastor and the church secretary. The operation of the dual file is a responsibility of a committee concerned with achieving the purposes of the church by recommending persons to occupy roles to achieve goals. The committee performs an advisory staff function through central records.

NOTES

NOTES

PREFACE

1. Herbert A. Thelen, *Dynamics of Groups at Work* (Chicago: University of Chicago Press, copyright 1954 by the University of Chicago), p. v. It is Professor Thelen's position that it is in the group that personality is modified and socialized; and further, that it is through the workings of groups that society is changed and adapted to its times.
2. *Ibid.*, p. v.
3. *Ibid.*, p. 67.
4. *Ibid.*
5. Gordon W. Allport, "The Psychology of Participation," in *Human Factors in Management* by Schuyler Dean Hoslett (New York: Harper & Brothers, 1946), p. 258.
6. Matthew 4:18–20.
7. Matthew 4:21–22.
8. Matthew 9:9.

CHAPTER 1

1. See J. F. Brown, *The Psychodynamics of Abnormal Behavior* (New York: McGraw-Hill Book Company, 1940), p. 138.
2. Rachel Henderlite, *A Call to Faith* (Richmond: John Knox Press, 1955), pp. 184–187.
3. James Moffatt, translator, *The Holy Bible* (New York: Harper & Brothers, 1926), I Corinthians 13:4–7.
4. See Talcott Parsons and Edward A. Shils, editors, *Toward a General Theory of Action* (Cambridge: Harvard University Press, 1951). In current thinking in human relations the role becomes the social unit. Relationships exist in action patterns; all terms refer to action. A social structure is thus made up of a network of positions (roles) which can be occupied by individuals or groups. A person taking a particular role must establish relationships with certain other specified individuals occupying related action roles, not as a matter of choice but through the demands of the social structure. The pattern of roles which constitutes the social structure links living persons with organizations and also links the people in an organization with one another. But roles are not people, and people are not roles. To roles are attached job responsibility and authority. Role relationships determine the official relationships possible among people, the

163

pattern of roles, and of relationships giving the formal setting in which working behavior takes place. For a detailed discussion of this concept, see Elliott Jaques, *The Changing Culture of a Factory* (London: Tavistock Publications, 1951), pp. 249–250.

5. Allport, "The Psychology of Participation," in *Human Factors in Management*, p. 258.

6. Gordon W. Allport, "A Psychological Approach to the Study of Love and Hate," in *Explorations in Altruistic Love and Behavior*, P. A. Sorokin, editor (Boston: Beacon Press, 1950), p. 164.

CHAPTER 2

1. Hugh Hartshorne, *Character in Human Relations* (New York: Charles Scribner's Sons, 1932).
2. *Ibid.*, p. 305.
3. *Ibid.*, p. 309.
4. *Ibid.*, p. 249.
5. *Ibid.*, p. 258.

CHAPTER 3

1. *Improving the Total Program of Your Church* (Chicago: National Council of Churches, copyright 1951 by the National Council of the Churches of Christ in the U.S.A.), p. 6.
2. Harold F. Smiddy, *General Electric's Philosophy and Approach for Management Development* (New York: American Management Association, 1955), p. 7.
3. See Judge Julius H. Miner, "Crime and Juvenile Delinquency," *American Bar Association Journal*, July, 1955, p. 601.
4. Sheldon and Eleanor Glueck, *Unraveling Juvenile Delinquency* (Cambridge: Harvard University Press, and Commonwealth Fund, New York, 1950), pp. 281–282.
5. Henderlite, *A Call to Faith*, p. 119.
6. *Ibid.*, p. 166.
7. John S. C. and Helen H. Kemp, *The Ministry of Music* (Oklahoma City: First Presbyterian Church). This 8-page folder provides one of the best examples of a policy statement issued by a local church.
8. Frank Wade Smith, *Leaders of Young People* (New York: The Methodist Book Concern, 1922), pp. 102–103.
9. Henderlite, *A Call to Faith*, pp. 195–201.

CHAPTER 4

1. James Reeves, editor, *The Holy Bible in Brief* (New York: Julius Messner, Inc., 1954), Foreword.
2. *The Pastor and Ways of Using the Bible*, pamphlet (New York: American Bible Society).
3. Murray G. Ross, *Religious Beliefs in Youth* (New York: Association Press, 1950), p. 70.

CHAPTER 5

1. See *Adult Leadership*, monthly publication of the Adult Education Association of the U.S.A., October, 1952.

CHAPTER 6

1. *Improving the Total Program of Your Church*, p. 6.
2. Thelen, *Dynamics of Groups at Work*, pp. 130–131.
3. John K. Hemphill, *Situational Factors in Leadership* (Columbus: Ohio State University, Bureau of Educational Research, 1949), pp. 30–37.
4. Thelen, *Dynamics of Groups at Work*, pp. 129–130.
5. *Ibid.*, p. 130.
6. Moffatt, translator, *The Holy Bible*, Matthew 9:12–13.
7. *Ibid.*, Matthew 12:7.
8. See J. F. Brown, *The Psychodynamics of Abnormal Behavior*, p. 179.

CHAPTER 7

1. Nathaniel Cantor, *Dynamics of Learning* (Buffalo: Foster & Stewart, 1950), p. 183.
2. For a general discussion of Role Playing, see Thelen, *Dynamics of Groups at Work*, pp. 192–201; and Alan F. Klein, *Role Playing* (New York: Association Press, 1956).
3. For a general discussion of the *Buzz Session*, see Thelen, *Dynamics of Groups at Work*, pp. 201–210.
4. *Ibid.*

CHAPTER 9

1. Thelen, *Dynamics of Groups at Work*, p. 296.
2. Hemphill, *Situational Factors in Leadership*, pp. 6, 100.
3. Harold F. Smiddy, *Integrating and Motivating for Effective Performance* (New York: General Electric Company, 1955), p. 7.
4. *Ibid.*, p. 13.
5. Thelen, *Dynamics of Groups at Work*, p. 307.
6. Col. Bernard S. Waterman, "Don't Let 'Management' Trick You," *The Army Combat Forces Journal*, September, 1955.
7. Lawrence K. Frank, *How to Be a Modern Leader* (New York: Association Press, 1954), p. 69.
8. Thelen, *Dynamics of Groups at Work*, p. 190.
9. *Ibid.*
10. Frank, *How to Be a Modern Leader*, p. 62.

APPENDIX I

1. Highet, Gilbert, *The Art of Teaching* (New York: Alfred A. Knopf, 1900), pp. 270–271, 280–281.

INDEX

A

B

C

D

E

F

G

H

I

J

K

L

M

N

O

P

V

W

Y